T0318503

Cambridge Elements

GEOPOLITICS OF DIGITAL HERITAGE

Natalia Grincheva
University of the Arts Singapore and The University of Melbourne
Elizabeth Stainforth
University of Leeds

Shaftesbury Road, Cambridge CB2 8EA, United Kingdom

One Liberty Plaza, 20th Floor, New York, NY 10006, USA

477 Williamstown Road, Port Melbourne, VIC 3207, Australia

314–321, 3rd Floor, Plot 3, Splendor Forum, Jasola District Centre, New Delhi – 110025, India

103 Penang Road, #05–06/07, Visioncrest Commercial, Singapore 238467

Cambridge University Press is part of Cambridge University Press & Assessment, a department of the University of Cambridge.

We share the University's mission to contribute to society through the pursuit of education, learning and research at the highest international levels of excellence.

www.cambridge.org
Information on this title: www.cambridge.org/9781009500142

DOI: 10.1017/9781009182072

When citing this work, please include a reference to the DOI 10.1017/9781009182072

First published 2024

A catalogue record for this publication is available from the British Library.

ISBN 978-1-009-50014-2 Hardback
ISBN 978-1-009-18208-9 Paperback
ISSN 2632-7074 (online)
ISSN 2632-7066 (print)

Geopolitics of Digital Heritage

Elements in Critical Heritage Studies

DOI: 10.1017/9781009182072
First published online: January 2024

Natalia Grincheva
University of the Arts Singapore and The University of Melbourne

Elizabeth Stainforth
University of Leeds

Author for correspondence: Natalia Grincheva,
natalia.grincheva@unimelb.edu.au

Abstract: *Geopolitics of Digital Heritage* analyses and discusses the political implications of the largest digital heritage aggregators across different scales of governance, from the city-state governed Singapore Memory Project, to a national aggregator like Australia's Trove, to supranational digital heritage platforms, such as Europeana, to the global heritage aggregator, Google Arts & Culture. These four dedicated case studies provide focused, exploratory sites for critical investigation of digital heritage aggregators from the perspective of their geopolitical motivations and interests, the economic and cultural agendas of involved stakeholders, as well as their foreign policy strategies and objectives. The Element employs an interdisciplinary approach and combines critical heritage studies with the study of digital politics and communications. Drawing from empirical case study analysis, it investigates how political imperatives manifest in the development of digital heritage platforms to serve different actors in a highly saturated global information space, ranging from national governments to transnational corporations.

This Element also has a video abstract: www.cambridge.org/geopolitics

Keywords: cultural heritage media, digital heritage, digital geopolitics, digital aggregators, space production

ISBNs: 9781009500142 (HB), 9781009182089 (PB), 9781009182072 (OC)
ISSNs: 2632-7074 (online), 2632-7066 (print)

Contents

1 Introduction

Over the past two decades, digital technology has fundamentally transformed the way cultural heritage is accessed and consumed. In the contemporary media environment, cultural heritage circulates on a global scale, becoming 'a mobile assemblage of things, dynamical processes and interactions characterized by functional flow, conflict, friction, intensities, turbulence and emergence' (Cameron and Mengler, 2015: 59). Moreover, contact with cultural heritage is underpinned by vast information infrastructures that enable data networking, storage and sharing. While they are usually invisible from the user perspective, practices such as mass digitization and aggregation have been recognized as defining concepts of our time (Bonde Thylstrup, 2018). There have even been calls for a 'global infrastructure for digital cultural heritage' (Povroznik, 2018). Such practices increasingly structure the way we speak, think about and engage with heritage.

This Element highlights a particular aspect of digital heritage, taking large-scale data aggregation as its focus. Aggregators are systems that collect, format and manage metadata from providers such as galleries, libraries, archives and museums (GLAMs), and offer federated access to that data via online portals and websites (Bettivia and Stainforth, 2019). Metadata refers to the descriptions of digital objects and records to facilitate their discovery in online archives. Drawing from Michel Foucault's understanding of the notion of the archive – first, as a more general epistemological category or knowledge production system; second, as a cultural and political reality marked by power dynamics – the Element defines digital aggregators as complex systems of 'utterability' which shape 'the law of what can be said', exhibited and displayed (Foucault, 2002: 186–188). Here, we analyse four of the largest and most well-established aggregators of cultural heritage data: the state-sponsored public crowdsourcing campaign, Singapore Memory Project; the National Library of Australia's Trove; the European Commission-funded Europeana, which connects 4,000 cultural institutions across Europe; and the biggest corporate aggregator in the world, Google Arts & Culture. The volume of digital heritage content they have managed to consolidate between them is staggering, amounting to hundreds of millions of items. This huge scale and reach have been achieved by government and corporate actors with political agendas and aspirations that impact heritage presentation in the international arena.

In line with Foucault's (2002) conceptualization of the archive as sociological phenomenon and a governmental technology, heritage is usually understood 'as a socio-political process that codifies and orders, preserves and exhibits, reconstructs and erases, and serves as a medium through which ideologies are both advanced and resisted' (Winter, 2023: 130). Chiara De Cesari proposes the term 'heritage regimes' to refer to a set of 'implicit or explicit principles, norms, rules, and decision-making procedures' that 'regulate areas of international relations', shaping politics of heritage discourses even on the transnational level (2013: 401). Likewise, digital heritage has been defined as a predominantly political concept and practice (McCrary, 2011; Winter, 2022a). These political dimensions have been studied in various ways and dispersed over professional and media boundaries (Lewi et al., 2020; Parry, 2010). Early research on the subject examined the influence of new and emerging digital media in museums and cultural heritage institutions (Parry, 2007, 2010). Fiona Cameron and Sarah Kenderdine (2007) were among the first to stress the need for a critical theorization of digital heritage and note its reshaping of political power in the cultural sector. Since then, the scholarship has expanded to include the impact of mass digitization projects (Bonde Thylstrup, 2018), the uses of big data in heritage (Bonacchi and Krzyzanska, 2019), and the role of heritage infrastructures in online environments (Freire et al., 2018; Lähdesmäki, 2019).

The critical turn in heritage studies (Harvey, 2001; Smith, 2006; Harrison, 2012) has brought to the fore the power dynamics of digital heritage regimes and the role of digital platforms in reproducing authorized heritage discourses (Taylor and Gibson, 2017; Bettivia and Stainforth, 2019). Recently, Tim Winter has started an important conversation on the 'geocultural power' of digital heritage, or the 'capacity to write and map geocultural histories' in light of digitization as 'the dramatic expansion in scale and volume brought by the digital, forg[ing] new pathways for knowledge production and affective dissemination' (Winter 2022a: 933). He interrogates how these geocultural histories 'are to be written, mapped and documented? And of course, by whom?' (Winter, 2022a: 934). Winter's research has important implications for digital heritage and how power is spatialized and distributed globally. This Element makes the case for the significance of digital heritage to contemporary geopolitics. It investigates how digital heritage aggregation emerges as an expression of geopolitical interests by state and non-state actors.

Defining the Geopolitics of Digital Heritage

The term 'geopolitics' was first coined in 1899 by Swedish professor of political science Rudolf Kjellen (Björk and Lundén 2021). He defined it as a new approach to international politics that emphasized the important role of geographical territory and natural resources in shaping competition between nation-states on the world stage. Geopolitics referred to strategic actions by national governments to secure their interests in the international arena. At the beginning of the twentieth century, the study of geopolitics attracted stronger academic attention, opening new avenues for a more in-depth investigation of the politics of geographical space and the allocation of valuable resources (Powers and Jablonski, 2015). However, the negative connotations of the term and its association with imperialism and social Darwinism were also consolidated. As such, the British geographer Halford Mackinder framed geopolitics in terms of a grand strategy of land-based and sea-based powers (Knutsen, 2014). This definition acquired even stronger significance during the Cold War when geopolitics mainly referred to great power rivalries and their territorial tensions, interventions, and struggles for ideological influence.

By the end of the twentieth century, geopolitics was severely criticized for serving the interests of major powers, as well as for focusing exclusively on nation-states as the main unit of analysis (Al-Rodhan, 2014). Moreover, the rapid advancement of digital communication technologies started to enable instant connectivity among different societies, challenging the terms of strict geographic borders and leading to the emergence of new multilateral institutions and non-state political actors (Kelley, 2014). Geopolitics in the digital era started to be defined by many actors, including large transnational media corporations, like Google and Facebook, regional or sub-state actors, digitally mobilized communities and even individuals or so-called influencers (Hulsman, 2019). These changes, accompanied by the rise of 'de-territorialized' threats and opportunities, pushed nation-states to increasingly operate beyond their immediate geographic territories. In the digital realm, cyber warfare, cyber-attacks, and cyber espionage started to create high-level political tensions and shaped international crises (Bjola and Pammen, 2019). Political mobilization, economic opportunities, and provision of national security migrated to the digital arena. As a result, social media mobilization and digital diplomacy started to play an increasingly significant role in world politics, where the position and power of different actors in the global information space define political outcomes (Bjola and Holmes, 2015).

Digital geopolitics is a new phenomenon that brings together two opposing trends. First, it involves the power politics of territorial units, including traditional nations or regional actors, that are increasingly operating in the digital domain. Second, it encompasses decentralized transnational networks and communities, as well as powerful non-state actors, including media giants with a reach far beyond politically fixed geography (Bendiek et al., 2019). While nation-states continue to hold military power, dominate macroeconomics, and decide on their own internal security, they also have to account for the influence and power of other actors and movements, unfolding in cyberspace

(Hulsman, 2019). Furthermore, their power positions and economic gains now directly depend on digital infrastructures and the capacity to 'globalize' their own technological systems to shape international standards, products, rules and even social norms and cultural values (Saran, 2020). As Peter Van Ham indicates, social power embedded in global perceptions 'has become an important factor in international politics, shaping expectations as well as policies' (2008: 240).

This position is based on earlier assumptions articulated by communication scholars (Ronfeldt and Arquilla, 1999; Castells, 2008), who have argued that in the twenty-first century, public opinion is a new superpower. This phenomenon could also be analysed through the lens of soft power, a concept coined by Joseph Nye. It refers to intangible forms of power such as culture, ideology, and institutions. In the context of the knowledge-based global economy, soft power is a more sophisticated tool to influence international politics, in contrast to military or economic coercion (Nye, 2004). A country can generate soft power if it can exploit culture, information, and technology to inhabit the mind space of another country. In terms of technology, digital geopolitics has become a new arena of political struggle, where information serves as a major weapon of power and control. Strategic constructions and manipulations of informational environments continually replace traditional principles of geopolitics, including military might or economic regulations (Ronfeldt and Arquilla, 2020). The global interconnectivity facilitated by digital technologies allows for the unlimited flow of cultural information, directly reaching people from different parts of the world (Potter, 2002). Strategic management of these global flows of information involves different actors in the culture wars for domination and control over human attention (Curtin and Gaither, 2007). As a result, in the digital age, power in the international arena depends on the actor's capacity to shape global informational environments, mobilize online publics, and manage cultural representations shaping human values and identities.

In this Element, we understand geopolitics as an interdisciplinary field of study combining knowledge across geography, political sciences, and international relations. Geography in this regard includes not only location or topography, but also elements of human and political geography, which in their turn encompass cultural boundaries, culturally significant and religious landmarks and sites that define the virtual borders of nation-states, communities and societies (Al-Rodhan, 2014). Colin Flint points out that 'geopolitics is not just a way of seeing. It is also the actions and outcomes that simultaneously transform spaces, places, and politics' (2017: 302). In his view, geopolitics constitutes both a practice and a representation (Flint, 2017: 36). As such, it is based on complex interrelationships between, on the one hand, physical space and, on the other, the conduct of foreign policy within this space that creates a new geographical representation of the world (Ó Tuathail and Agnew, 1992).

Scholars of critical geopolitics (Ó Tuathail, 2005; Agnew, 2007) have divided geopolitical studies into 'formal' geopolitics, based on theories and doctrines, 'practical' geopolitics including official documents, and so-called 'popular' geopolitics. The latter refers to a way of imagining geopolitics and expressing it through popular culture, mass media, and everyday communication (Dijkink, 1998; Dittmer and Bos, 2019). However, the digital era's impact on global communications and politics has compressed three different dimensions into one. Jason Dittmer and Nicholas Gray (2010) suggest that digital geopolitics emerges at the crossroads of formal, practical, and popular geopolitics. As a form of cultural representation, digital heritage sits at the intersection of the popular and the political. Winter's notion of geocultural power describes aspects of this phenomenon and its ability 'to advance values and ideals' as an 'architecture for norm setting and advancing particular worldviews that are deployed to impose a sense of directionality on international affairs' (2022b: 394). Moreover, as Daniel Herwitz observes, 'political history is itself an object of heritage making' (2012: 3). Understanding the political past and present is in many cases shaped by a set of heritage artefacts, exhibitions, and collections that constitute the cultural memory and legacy of an individual society or community. 'Justice becomes, in the realm of heritage making, a new kind of contest between storytelling, medium, and power. Heritage is a window into the relation of aesthetics to politics' (Herwitz, 2012: 3).

Indeed, the ability of digital heritage to represent history, environments, and values 'makes it possible to manipulate the information in both spatial and temporal ways, then transmit it to remote viewers' (Kalay et al., 2007: 3). Digital re-presentations provide a new form for cultural heritage and consequently invite new interpretations, which have very strong geopolitical implications (Kalay et al., 2007). While human life remains tied to specific spaces, times and places, representations created by digital heritage media change the ways in 'which space, time and place themselves appear, and are understood, and so too, the way in which human existence appears, is understood, and is experienced' (Malpas, 2007: 19). One of the key tasks of heritage sites, either physical or digital, is helping audiences to engage meaningfully with them. Yet, as Jeff Malpas points out, it is questionable whether digital heritage enables 'greater engagement with the site or the artefact as such, or it, instead, enables a greater level of engagement only with the reproduced site or artefact' (2007: 20), which is already heavily charged with new political meanings and interpretations.

Digital heritage, by virtue of how it is collected and displayed, destroys heritage artefacts' sense of being in place. This 'shifts away from the particular place through which a singular encounter with the work is possible, towards a generic and uniform space that enables a universal accessibility of the artwork from anywhere within that space' (Malpas, 2007: 21). Through becoming something more generic, digital heritage evokes the obliteration of place. In the dissolution of the near and far in relation to heritage objects, audiences also lose a sense of the near and far in relation to themselves (Malpas, 2007), making this 'empty shell' vulnerable to occupation by new political meanings. In the same manner as the curation of physical cultural heritage objects, digital heritage presents a range of critical issues to be resolved in relation to authenticity, censorship, image manipulation, and ideological control (McCrary, 2011).

The Production and Deconstruction of Digital Heritage Geopolitics

The Element reveals and explores the affordances and implications of digital heritage through the practice of digital heritage aggregation. Here, aggregators are positioned as 'history machines' that do not merely preserve and share in digital form the cultural heritage of societies but, in fact, construct new temporal and spatial realities. The 'epistemic' nature of heritage data and, more importantly, its ability to be digitally organized and re-interpreted through different representations is what makes it political. It becomes critical in geopolitical terms, especially when it concerns cultural and political borders, contested territories, cross-cultural engagements, and proximities as dimensions of political geographies. As such, digital heritage aggregators are vehicles for shifting epistemic paradigms, eliding, or constructing the cultural identities of communities.

Understanding digital heritage aggregators as 'an impressive array of simulacra, instantaneous communication, ubiquitous media, and global interconnectedness' (Cameron and Kenderdine, 2007), the Element explores relationships between geopolitics and the digital geographies and memories constructed by heritage media. Following De Cesari's (2013) identification of heritage regimes, which constitute both the field of government and dimensions of international relations, and Winter's concept of geocultural power, this Element explores how culture, history and memory are organized through digital heritage aggregators in ways that exert power, 'both within the confines of the nation-state and, crucially, beyond it' (2021: 1392). Geopolitics here consists of different forms of heritage governance, from state actors, like Australia's Trove and Singapore Memory Project to intergovernmental actors, like Europeana, to the corporate deployment of neoliberal state extensions, as with Google Arts & Culture. *Specifically, the monograph interrogates how these different actors shape the geopolitical representation of space, through digital heritage aggregation, and how the production of digital heritage shapes the political agenda of involved actors on the global map.* Digital heritage in this way is understood as the main means by which cultural and political geographies are coded and depicted.

For example, on the one hand, digital heritage has been an important tool for state-driven expressions of national unity and nation-building, nurturing a sense of empowerment and belonging (Grincheva, 2012; Herwitz, 2012; Winter, 2022a). Being trans-territorial and translocal, digital heritage can communicate nationalistic narratives which acquire potency through their global circulation (Mankekar, 1999). They play a crucial role in 'the creation and promulgation of nationalist affects' (Punathambekar and Mohan, 2019: 205). In this sense, the cases of Australia's Trove and Singapore Memory Project aim to reveal specific strategies of digital national space construction, especially when they concern the establishment of national digital legitimacy and sovereignty. On the other hand, digital representations of heritage dramatically expand the scope of heritage regimes enacted by 'new forms of transnational, neoliberal, and non-state governmentality' (De Cesari, 2020: 31). These representations enable the process of 'globalizing the local, packaging it in a common and neutral language with immediate status and recognition value on the global stage' (Herwitz, 2012: 5). This entry into the circuit of the global media space of the 'heritage ecotourism market' offers 'global comprehensibility and recognition' and makes local heritage objects 'globally comprehensible, consumable items' (Herwitz, 2012: 5). The case of Europeana is illustrative here because it aggregates heritage across thousands of museums in Europe, removing it from local historical, cultural, and linguistic contexts and bringing it 'under one roof' in the European project.

Finally, the global media space has started to witness the phenomenon of 'media imperialism' (Mirrlees, 2013) or 'platform imperialism' (Jin, 2017), whereby a handful of digital media companies have become powerful actors who shape the everyday social, cultural, and political lives of people all over the world. Their geopolitical ambitions are manifested in the creation of global markets of media consumption. Digital heritage 'disneyfication' or commodification through their platforms give rise to new imaginative, globally converged geographies of heritage experiences, which lose their sense of place and time (Malpas, 2007). The case of Google Arts & Culture aims to explore the digital geopolitical dimension of these processes, exposing and revealing the obstacles, challenges, and possibilities redefining global heritage geographies by powerful new actors on the world stage.

All four case studies in this Element interrogate digital representations of geographical space and their geopolitical characteristics. 'Since space is the ontological core of geopolitics' (Turčalo and Kulović, 2018: 18), we view digital heritage aggregators' production of space predominantly as a geopolitical statement, intervening in mainstream global discourses and international relations. Following the tradition of 'popular' geopolitics, the volume understands the concept of space either as representative of geopolitical situations or as a stage on which human action is performed (Kaplan, 2012). The Element questions: What are the geopolitical motivations of the representation of space produced by digital heritage aggregators? Who benefits from this and who is affected by the geopolitical narratives of digital heritage aggregators?

These questions inform the inquiry, which is undertaken on two interrelated levels of analysis: **(1) a power-critical perspective** of space that concerns policies and regulations enabling normalization processes in spatial construction through differentiations, attributions of meaning or hierarchizations; and **(2) a heritage media-oriented perspective**, which analyses heritage aggregators as projectors of spatialized power, while themselves being identified as virtual spaces. Research was carried out by the authors in different parts of the world from North America (USA and Canada) to Europe and Asia Pacific, including Australia and Singapore as places of research residencies. The authors conducted semi-structured interviews with professionals involved in the case study projects, as well as staff from participating GLAMs, to gain insights into the motivations for large-scale data aggregation from an organizational viewpoint. These interview accounts were instrumental to complement and deepen the desk research on existing (inter)national discourses of digital heritage politics, conducted through a focused analysis of policy documents, strategic reports, and websites across countries. The digital site of inquiry focused on contextual observations of the heritage aggregators – their online design, architecture, content, and operations – in order to deconstruct their geopolitical meanings and orientations.

This methodological approach and analysis of four case studies revealed that space-related differentiations inform (self-)positionings, 'imaginative geographies' (Said, 1978), as well as constructing identities and 'imagined communities' (Anderson, 1983). Digital heritage media thus constitute spaces of human memory and identity apparent in their differentiations, border crossings, inclusions, and exclusions. All the case studies engage closely with issues of memory and heritage production and interrogate their meaning in the context of digital heritage aggregation. Considering that a phenomenology of remembrance is implicated in the dynamics of digital representations, each project – Singapore Memory Project, Trove, Europeana, and Google Arts &

Culture – demonstrates how these dynamics surface in the interfaces, design, content, and functionality of aggregators and how digital technologies of memory shape global media spaces.

Section Outline

The Element is divided into five sections, focusing on each of the case studies. Section 2 introduces the Singapore Memory Project (SMP), a Government campaign to bring together heritage institutions, communities, and publics through crowdsourcing national culture, memory and identity. Launched in 2011, SMP aimed to collect and preserve Singapore's culture, heritage, and history, as well as promoting it globally for discovery and tourism. The section investigates the geopolitical context of Singapore, its national ambitions and concerns in the wider Asia-Pacific region. It reveals how the management of SMP turned the public crowdsourcing campaign into a Government tool of nation-building, at the same time as it enacted a strategy of virtual enlargement for global audiences.

Section 3 looks at Trove and interrogates the geopolitical implications of digital heritage as a projection of national culture. Managed by the National Library of Australia (NLA), Trove is positioned both as a means of promoting Australian heritage regionally and internationally, and as a way of mediating and giving expression to the diverse narratives of the Australian people. The section analyses the contradictions at play in the digital heritage of Trove, especially with regard to how the history of the nation is contested by the claims of First Nations Australians. The concept of Indigenous geopolitics is used to provide a counterpoint to the presentation of a unified national culture and draw attention to the limits of inclusion in government-affiliated projects.

Section 4 turns to Europeana, arguing that it has been motivated by the geopolitical goal of constructing a heritage culture in the virtual domain of European identity. The project is revealing of present-oriented interests that centre on the idea of European culture as a destination point and a marker for greater social and political cohesion. In tandem with this move towards constituting a coherent transnational identity, Europeana has also been increasingly aligned with the EU's agenda to achieve digital sovereignty through the creation of protected 'data spaces'. The section shows that cultural heritage is instrumentalized in Europeana as a method of social integration, at the same time as it reflects the geopolitical aspirations of the EU to become a global economic sovereign power.

Section 5 shifts from aggregators devised as national or supranational governmental heritage sites, to a global heritage platform developed by the largest transnational media corporation in the world, Google. It explores the geopolitics of Google Arts & Culture (GAC), against a backdrop of the digitization, globalization, and decentralization of state powers. Google is identified as a new economic actor on the world stage, and GAC's ambition to bring 'the world's art and culture online for everyone' (GAC, 2022b) is recognized as a dimension of Google's platform imperialism. The section considers the implications of mass heritage aggregation in light of Google's global activities, geopolitical agenda, and impact on global consumption of digital heritage that goes beyond the merely economic.

The Element positions digital heritage geopolitics as a new field of academic inquiry. It offers compelling case studies and insightful analysis to identify and describe different strategies of geopolitical space production via the media of digital heritage. Through these explorations it interrogates the future of mass digital heritage aggregation on different levels of implementation, from the urban in the case of Singapore Memory Project, to the national, as in Australia's Trove, to the regional in Europeana, and finally to the global as exemplified in the GAC platform.

2 Crowdsourcing National Identity: Singapore Memory Project

Introduction

Everyone who comes to Singapore, a small city-state island located off the southern tip of the Malay Peninsula in Southeast Asia, is dazzled with its developed urban modernity, economic prosperity, innovative technological design, and the highly multicultural composition of its residents. Limited by a total area of less than a thousand square kilometres, the island is home to five and a half million people, largely comprising the country's three main ethnic groups – Chinese, Malays, Indians – as well as immigrants from all over the world (Department of Statistics Singapore, 2022). Characterized by a strong system of governance, a robust fiscal infrastructure, and a secure position in global markets, in the fifty years since independence from Britain, Singapore has quickly developed into what has been described as a postcolonial 'economic miracle' (Barr and Skrbiš, 2011).

Now the city is known globally as 'a highly competitive, cutting-edge society where efficiency reigns' (King, 2008: 13) with one of the highest GDP rates per capita in the world (WB, 2022). As part of its development in the last decades, Singapore has embraced new technology, the creative economy, and the heritage tradition of mixing 'the East and the West . . . as a way of harnessing the region's unique distinctiveness and promoting its renewed vitality' (Yue, 2006: 17). Remarkably, only five years after the global development of the World Wide

Web in 1995, Singapore attained the title of 'intelligent island', through its scheme to grant Singaporeans a universal Internet connection for various social and commercial purposes, via an island-wide cable network (Lee, 2012: 107). Amid these fast-paced developments, though, there has been a growing awareness amongst the Government and citizens of the need to create a sense of belonging and preserve the history of such a young nation, culminating 'in the genesis of the Singapore Memory Project (SMP), a national memory initiative' (Tang, 2013: 2).

Starting with a series of events entitled Heritage Roadshow in 2006, modelled after the British television programme Antiques Roadshow (Pin, 2014), the SMP grew into a nationwide campaign, led by the Singapore Ministry of Information, Communications and the Arts and facilitated by the National Library Board (NLB). It officially started in 2011 with an ambitious goal to collect five million memories, one memory for every resident, until 2015, when Singapore would mark fifty years of independence. The project was announced by the Prime Minister of Singapore, Mr Lee Hsien Loong, during the 2011 National Day Rally, considered to be the most important speech of the year. Lee (2011) emphasized that the memories 'can come from anybody, any person, any community, any organization or institution which has experienced Singapore' to capture the stories of real people and to 'weave the tapestry of the nation'. The SMP went on to become the largest digital heritage crowdsourcing project in the history of the island, designed to collect, preserve, celebrate, and share Singapore's culture and history. Initiated through handwritten memories, acquisition via roadshows and community events, the portal SingaporeMemory.SG was developed for digital ingestion of transcribed memory cards, collected from older generations.

Inviting 'every Singaporean to own a memory account to deposit their memories', the portal was intended to build a repository of national memory and make it available to wider global audiences for discovery and research. This memory bank aspired to feature 'recollections of historical events, documentation of recent events of significance, as well as personal memories of people, places and activities that resonate with the Singapore psyche' (Ng, 2011). The project encouraged individuals, communities, groups, and institutions of Singapore to contribute their personal stories in the form of text, images, or videos to the portal to build 'a culture of remembering, which will nurture bonding and rootedness' (SMP, n.d.). The portal was also accompanied by an iPhone application to enable people to dynamically capture and instantly upload memories. Furthermore, the SMP launched numerous engagement campaigns facilitated through various social media channels, including irememberSG Facebook page, @irememberSG Twitter and Instagram as well as the iremember.sg blog. The decision of the NLB to reach out to the larger communities of Singapore netizens was strategic. At the time the project was launched, Singapore society had one of the highest literacy rates in the world of 96.1 per cent (WB, n.d.a). It also remained the most connected city, with almost three in four people owning a smartphone and over 70 per cent of households with Internet access (WB, n.d.b). 'In that context, it was quite natural that the SMP would have an online and social media component to it', that was even 'positioned as a complementary extension to collect memories online' (Chew and Jailan, 2013: 357).

Partnering with 218 organizations, including the National Archives of Singapore, Singapore Press Holdings, the libraries of the Institute of Southeast Asian Studies, the National University of Singapore, and the Composers and Authors Society of Singapore, the SMP also drew on support of 188 Memory Corps, volunteers who collected memories from communities, drove memory campaigns and recruited memory donors locally and from overseas. The SMP Director Gene Tan (2012) once shared that the project stemmed from the bureaucracy of the state 'trying to create a stage in which all memories will come together' to develop a 'grand narrative' and 'construct a version of Singapore'. Indeed, from October 2009, when the Steering Committee of the project was officially formed, various stakeholders committed to take an active part in safeguarding the documentation of the heritage and cultural memory of Singapore. These included Government agencies as wide-ranging as the Ministry of Defence, the Media Development Authority, the National Arts Council, the Urban Redevelopment Authority, the Housing Development Board, and the Public Utilities Board, as well as key national heritage agencies, including the National Archives and the National Heritage Board and Asian Film Archives (Foo et al., 2010).

This top-down approach, in the words of the Prime Minister, gave birth to 'the soul of the nation' and ensured that the unveiling of the SMP presented a coordinated and accurately executed nationwide campaign to create a grand narrative (Lee, 2011). While the inclusion of crowdsourced content aspired to share a 'real history written in people's everyday lives' (Ismail, 2013), the project was not necessarily concerned with creating an alternative narrative to the state vision, but instead to 'complement the Singapore Story' (Lee, 2011). What purposes did this public spectacle serve and what kind of geopolitical motivations drove the development of this digital heritage aggregator? This section argues that the SMP was developed to pursue two key geopolitical objectives: first, to legitimize Singapore as a nation; second, to reinforce its regional and global position and 'brand' in the Asia-Pacific region, as a small, but powerful, city-state on the crossroads of the East and the West.

Nation-Building: From Singapore Production to Consumption

As a young postcolonial state that only gained independence from Britain in 1965 through an expulsion from Malaysia after an unsuccessful merger, Singapore desperately needed to create a national historical narrative 'as a means to justifying its existence' (Heng and Aljunied, 2009: 22). The nation-building project of Singapore as a sovereign country started with 'building the material fabric to fill the hollow shell of the state', focusing on building roads, factories, industries, armies, institutions of governance, and other urban infrastructure. This construction process, performed along the vertical axis between the people and the Government, developed a solid 'soft authoritarian' regime with a free market economy but strong social control (Roy, 1994). While rapidly progressing in its industrialization, Singapore struggled 'to provide a repertoire upon which to build the common foundations for national imagination' (Barr and Skrbiš, 2011). Originally known as a 'cultural desert', in the latest stages of its development, driven exclusively by pragmatism, Singapore embraced the creative economy to grow its own culture, but this mainly served as 'a practical resource' (Yue, 2006: 19). Singapore's nation-building project also provided the appropriate groundwork for the practice of Singapore citizenship, defined by Hill and Lian (2016) in the following way:

> Singapore citizenship is about being accepted as a privileged member of a multiracial, multicultural, multilingual, and multireligious community in return for one's tacit agreement to play a part in contributing actively to the – mostly economic – welfare of the nation. (130)

However, a nation-building project resting only on the ideological foundations of economic development, modernity and progress, and multiracialism could not be relied upon as a long-term resource. Recognizing this as a weak basis upon which to build nationhood, the Government faced a need to 'add to a sense of place, community, belonging and opportunity' (MCCY, 2013:16) and create a Singaporean identity, 'not singular and definitely not simplistic but definitely multifaceted', integrating many migrant communities to make 'Singapore a kaleidoscope of individuals, people, places and cultures' (Foo et al., 2010: 34). For instance, back in 2003, the Government-commissioned report 'Changing Mindsets, Deepening Relationships' specifically advised Singaporeans to express themselves socially, culturally, and artistically, and suggested the Government create more spaces to 'participate meaningfully in national and community life' (RSC, 2003: 20).

'A one-team regime that has won every election since 1965' (Heng and Aljunied, 2009: 11), the country approached the project of writing the

Singapore Story through its usual 'constructionist disposition towards governmental policies' (Barr and Skrbiš, 2011). Specifically, the nation-building project unveiled through national heritage institutions, which devised the SMP, was guided by several foundational principles. For example, the NLB, the official home of the project, emphasized the following objectives: (1) preventing 'the permanent loss of the nation's heritage, its roots and nation-building history', capturing the lives of the older generation who possessed first-hand accounts of Singapore's nation-building years; (2) changing 'the way in which people valued and paid emphasis to things of the past and to the experiences they had'; and (3) building a collective culture and identity (Pin, 2014). In this way, the project aimed to engage Singaporeans in the shared activity of remembering, to create 'a single national identity', imagined by the Singapore Tourism Board back in 2000, as proudly regarding oneself 'as a Singaporean first before a Chinese, Malay, Indian or Eurasian' (STB, 2000: 15). One critique of this 'Singaporeaness' is that it has been generated in the modernizing country through New Asian capitalist materialism, in which the knowledge economy, information regulation, and censorship produce citizens-as-consumers. Here, consumption is driven by a top-down policy climate, where citizenship can be merely expressed by 'a consumption of place' (Yue, 2006: 24). This place consumption framework is particularly important for Singapore. Historically, its population was composed almost entirely of migrants who kept very strong emotional linkages back to the lands of their origin, but who needed to be 're-engineered into a solitary, highly efficient and productive workforce' (Heng and Aljunied, 2009: 25).

In this scenario, the SMP aimed to reinforce the sense of geospatial belonging and strategically unveiled the memory collection endeavour through various campaigns associated with a celebration of the island's places, buildings, and locations. More than half of over fifty memory campaigns were devoted to Singapore city districts, famous buildings, and local communities. Some examples include 'I Remember Chestnut Estate', a city centre land space 'owned by a Eurasian family, the Boswells'; 'I remember goes to Punggol', a residential area in Singapore with a freshly constructed New Punggol Town, built on the former villages of the first Malay fishermen, which existed more than 200 years ago; 'irememberChinatown' and 'irememberVictoria', the famous Victoria Theatre and Concert Hall; and 'irememberMerlion', the local legend and globally recognized icon. One of the most important memory campaigns was the SG50 signature programme 'SG Heart Map' that 'brought Singaporeans together to share stories of the most endearing places' (SMP, 2015). It was promoted as 'the first-ever crowd-sourced map of the nation's 'heart' and special moments', which inspired seven lead artists to co-create works of art with local communities to showcase the stories contributed to SG Heart Map during the SG Heart Map Festival @ Float.

Collected for half a year, 100,000 contributions shared 'cherished places in Singapore relating to childhood, special moments, favourite hangouts and food places' (SMP, 2015). Featured on the top fifty SMP list as favourite 'Hang-Out' places for leisure, food, and shopping were Gardens by the Bay, Little India, Resorts World Sentosa, Changi Village, Chinese Garden, Marina Bay, Merlion Park, Raffles Place, River Safari, and Singapore Zoo. These perfectly matched the most visited tourist destinations promoted in all travel guides to Singapore. In this sense, the SG Heart Map presented the metropolis as a natural reality for consumption, building a narrative of 'spectacular populism', with the aim of being remembered as such (Goh, 2013). This construction of the urban spatial image, associated directly with the Singapore identity and national sense of belonging, does not challenge the global-local dynamic of the metropolis itself and does not attempt to 'intervene into the rhythmic heart at the core of the politics of memory' (Goh, 2013: 24). The SMP excellently mirrors the real urban identity of Singapore, purposefully designed to showcase a triumphant trajectory of progress.

The careful and strategic Government-led curation of urban heritage spaces has focused mostly on telling a Singapore Story of remarkable development, from a mere British colony to the most economically advanced city in Asia. Such heritage curation, though, requires a reification of heritage, which in many cases implies 'hiding' or redesigning some 'inconvenient' urban spaces and even 'forgetting micro-vernacular local meanings' (Liew et al., 2014: 265). For instance, the most recent victims of heritage demolition for the sake of modernization – including the old National Library and several eco-heritage areas, like the former Malayan Railway line or the Bukit Brown Cemetery – provide good examples of Singapore losing meaningful sites of historical identification (Liew et al., 2014). However, many of these historically meaningful places, which strongly resonate with the public urban experiences of the past, remain excluded from the SMP state-sponsored marketing platform of national glory.

Instead, the SMP celebrates top tourist locations and festivities through city-wide, incentivized community engagement initiatives, facilitated and moderated by the NLB. From 2011–2020, the NLB organized around fifty-two campaigns which aimed to 'tap into Singaporeans' nostalgia for the past' (Tang, C., 2013) and, in this way, controlled the public effort to share personal stories, memories, ideas, and values. Campaigns such as 'Reflections on our National Pledge', 'A Tribute to Our Pioneer Generation', 'Hands that brought us up', 'The Singapore Story: My Heart, My Hope, My Home', and many others were widely promoted within Singapore's public spaces. The SMP tapped into the national networks of public libraries located all over Singapore, to serve as memory collection points for the public. The results of such geographic reach can be seen in the project's uptake. For instance, the 2012 campaign 'My Library My Home' collected more than 57,000 cards from local communities (Tang, 2013). The SMP was also enthusiastically promoted via larger-scale state carnivals and events in different neighbourhoods across the island and almost all of them included monetary incentives or contests with prizes. The 2011 National Day Parade Organising Committee amassed 126,000 memory cards alone to contribute to the memory portal (Tang, 2013). Additionally, all the campaigns were supported through volunteers on site, distributing memory cards and encouraging people to participate. They recorded short oral history interviews and transcribed or scanned thousands of handwritten memory cards to be catalogued with metadata for the web portal.

By absorbing micro memories into the infrastructure of the dominant narrative, all these campaigns devised by state heritage institutions and their official partners, perfectly accorded with the Singapore Story, the grand narrative of the 'progress from third world to first through good governance and communitarian "Asian values," with the living memories of real people who experienced [. . .] this remarkable development' (Cheng, 2018: 68). Before a frustrating point was reached in 2013, when it became clear that collecting 5 million memories was not an achievable goal, quantity was paramount for the SMP. As a result, anything collected through the campaigns or city events would be uploaded, no matter how trivial, mundane, or insignificant these memories were. For example, schools were heavily involved in contributing to the portal by writing memory cards in class, which significantly added to the total count as they offered access to target groups who could be relied upon for massive participation.

Cheng (2018) analysed one of the numerous contributions to the 'irememberSchoolDays' campaign, organized by Nanyang Girls' High School (NYGH), which aimed to collect heart-warming stories and fond memories from students, teachers, and alumni. In NYGH, the graduating students shared a 'message of love' to their school through 600 written stories, drawings, and photographs, compiled in colourful scrapbooks collectively titled 'Messages from our hearts'. Among cards with students' messages of appreciation and love for their school, there were also anonymous cards that simply stated on otherwise blank pages, 'this is my d o o d l e' or 'You shouldn't be looking at this' in a tiny font making it illegible. These messages, as well as thousands of meaningless text comments like 'I love my school' or 'I love Singapore', perfectly manifested the acts of 'non-participation': doodling as 'the embodiment of not paying attention', or passive protests towards mandatory engagement (Cheng, 2018). These doodle comments also point to the degree of self-censorship and Government control over the public, even in their own cultural expressions. Indeed, Singaporeans are often described as 'living in a socially engineered and "selfcensorious" climate of fear' (Gomez, 2000: 9).

In the same way as parades and carnivals, which were also appropriated by the project as spaces for memory collection, the SMP, as a form of cultural popularization, effectively mobilized the people to support the Government-led initiative. As a discursive symbol of nationhood, the public 'consumption' of the SMP raised the 'national' consciousness of a communitarian culture and one 'that is likely to find little resistance' (Chua, 2006: 12). The majority of submitted stories fail to communicate anything more than sentimentality and nostalgia for vanishing urban-scapes of Singapore in its constant historical transformation from Third World to First World country (Liew and Pang, 2015). This nostalgia could be understood as preservation of the past in a very selective way by sentimentalizing, romanticizing, and even silencing more inconvenient memories. Focusing on the description of disappeared urban public spaces, contributors to the Government-sponsored SMP shied away from discussing political history in an honest critical manner, or offering critiques of past Government actions.

The memory portal did not invite more difficult memories that could reflect or question the Singapore Story through a counter-narrative, public concerns, or discussions of controversial moments in the history of the state. As some critics observe, the SMP does not include memories of the famous Singapore Bus Riots, the history of the merger with Malaysia and many other difficult historical moments (Blackburn, 2013). Indeed, back in 2012 when Gene Tan, the SMP Director, was challenged with a question about potential 'blank pages' of Singapore's history that the portal was not covering, he masterfully redirected the conversation to the future of Singapore: 'The national mood right now is that not so many people want to discuss the sensitive moments of history, but there is a lot of anxiety about where the country is going' and 'whether we are losing something important, what it means to be a Singaporean'.

Jumping to 2022 and doing a quick SMP search on the most pressing current issues of Singapore cultural life, the results remain disappointing. For example, in 2021 the arts community was shocked by the decision of the National Arts Council to remove the home premises of Singapore's first independent art space, the Substation, to renovate the building, making it another victim of non-stop development and modernization. Founded in 1990, the Substation has nurtured several generations of the most acclaimed Singapore artists and earned a reputation as a liberating and experimental artistic incubator space (Wang, 2022).

Despite debates about the Council's controversial decision taking place in artistic circles, as well as key cultural institutions and even the media, the SMP portal does not have a single record of the situation. This supports early observations about the SMP, made by Tan (2016), who described it as a highly ritualized platform 'that rides the wave of nostalgia and depoliticises the past in a renewed and seemingly more inclusive version and performance of The Singapore Story', while also hiding difficult pages of the national history (244). As Blackburn (2013) points out, this spectacle of nostalgia, divorced from Singapore's real history, appeared to many as tiring, prosaic, and trivial.

Nation Branding: Virtual Enlargement of Singapore

The suggestion that the SMP was designed to showcase, rather than to preserve, is evident in the fact that it contains memories of those contributors who do not necessarily belong to Singapore. Overseas Singaporeans and non-citizens were invited to participate in this project that welcomed 'tourists, Permanent Residents, students, businesspeople and various travellers who pass by each year' (Chew and Jailan, 2013: 355). As the SMP Assistant Director Wan Wee Pin confirmed, 'citizenship was not a prerequisite for participation in SMP', 'everyone who has passed through Singapore are welcome to share their memories' (Pin, 2013). In the interview he explained that the SMP was much more than a national project, it was 'very porous', inclusive and welcoming to the extent of accepting foreigners' memories of Singapore as 'relevant' and as valuable contributions to the national history (2012). For instance, in March 2013, the SMP was featured in the *New Straits Times* of Malaysia by Associate Editor and writer Fauziah Ismail, who described how she was approached by the project to pledge her personal blog posts where she shared some memories of Singapore (Pin, 2014). Her news article praised the SMP for such inclusiveness, complimenting the Singapore Government 'in preserving history in whatever form it comes in' (Ismail, 2013), thus serving as free promotion for Singapore in Malaysia.

By recruiting SMP contributors from overseas, the project extended its geography far beyond the island's borders and reached out to engage 'anyone who has ever experienced Singapore' (Pin, 2014: 67). This extension perfectly resembles the geopolitical strategy of virtual enlargement that is usually adopted by so-called 'small states' with limited resources and capabilities, to strengthen their global positions on the world stage and emphasize their legitimacy and competitiveness (Chong, 2010). For example, in the implementation of its global ambitions the National Heritage Board of Singapore (2008) stressed that 'it will take much more for a small nation like Singapore to stand out amidst the international competition for recognition and resources. It will take even more for heritage-related initiatives, which typically form a small part of the economy, to stand out' (10). A small state within its specific geostrategic and geo-economic realities usually faces trade-offs when engaging with big powers to secure its neutrality and balance relations (Rahman, 2020). Virtual enlargement strategy is based on extrapolating the state's actual power through virtual projections in terms of augmenting the potential of their political economy, models of good governance, or diplomatic mediation (Chong, 2010).

Specifically, Singapore aspires to demonstrate its regional leadership by 'transcending its geographical destiny' and 'enhancing its global brand as a good international citizen, albeit not one without envy from its regional neighbours' (Chong, 2010: 402). Indeed, the SMP Director shared that the 'NLB has been seen as a leader in the world of libraries and as a major magnet for educational trips around the world'. He stressed that the SMP has become an exemplar project, showcasing heritage web 2.0 best practice and receiving 'a lot of admiration in Asia, with many attempts to emulate this initiative' (Tan, 2013). Tan (2012) even designated a diplomatic role to the SMP 'as a soft power tool', exactly because 'of the very human personal component of the project'. According to the Director, the SMP serves as the perfect platform to establish and reinforce links within the region and across the world. Tapping into Singapore's already existing population diversity and inviting contributors to 'trace their roots', the ambition that the SMP aspires to is to represent 'all these cultural exchanges and international influences' (Tan, 2013). In this way, the project offers a convenient playground for exercising virtual enlargement that works through strategic multilateralism or projection of multilateralism by building on its multicultural social and historical roots.

As the SMP official rhetoric signals, with the development of digital technologies, Singapore has acquired additional tools for its virtual enlargement. In 2010, the Heritage Board explicitly articulated the need to develop 'virtual archives' which can allow the country to 'reach a wider audience locally and internationally as well as to lengthen the display period of its shows' (NHB, 2010: 1). Singapore has been quick in utilizing the potential of new media to offer new services and experiences to its audience. With an already established presence on the web through portals such as MyStory, a community wiki to post family memories, or Singapore Family Tree, a genealogy portal connecting Singaporeans 'past and present, local and overseas' (NHB, 2008: 28), the SMP emerged as the next step in Singapore's digital heritage promotion. Not only did the project utilize new technologies to demonstrate the innovative, web 2.0 heritage preservation expertise of Singapore, the participatory crowdsourcing nature of the project was also a response to twenty-first-century global audience demands for increased interactivity. To justify its status as a regional leader and be recognized as an 'innovator', Singapore needed to align with international best practices and meet global expectations of local-global reconciliatory policies for international familiarity and standardization (Chong, 2005: 559).

In 2012, for instance, the Government admitted that much of Singapore's cultural development was perceived locally and globally 'as being directed "top-down"', with a growing need to have 'more space and support to initiate artistic and cultural activities from the ground-up' (MCCY, 2013: 18). Comparing the project with similar initiatives in other countries, the SMP Assistant Director shared that the project was strategically presented as 'a ground-up initiative to give ordinary people a voice and offer them an opportunity to speak out and share their memories' (Pin, 2013). A strong authoritarian regime with draconian censorship regulations, Singapore, which has been dubbed 'Disneyland with the death penalty' (Gibson, 1993), strives to earn its global legitimacy by adapting to international norms. The SMP has been an opportunity for the country to demonstrate its support for democratic participation of the public in the nationwide campaign of memory preservation. It basically communicated a more emotive, participatory, and bottom-up approach to heritage-sharing and consumption that would 'appeal to a more sophisticated and globalised citizenry', 'based on the consumerist logic of a more self-indulgent middle class' (Tan, 2016: 244). This strategic focus, not only on the local but also on the global audience, is not surprising in the geopolitical context of Singapore. With its colonial legacies and limited natural resources, the island has always depended on global markets for its economic survival.

The internationalization of Singapore's economy and citizenry and positioning the city-state as a so-called 'global city' started as early as the 1960s (Chong, 2005). With the global emergence of creative economies, Singapore focused its efforts on its cultural industries, aiming to transform into a 'Global City for the Arts' (STPB & MIA, 1995). The rapid development of arts policies and cultural industries, spearheaded by the Government in the past thirty years, was geared towards positioning Singapore as a premier cultural hub regionally and internationally (Kawasaki, 2004). The National Arts Council (2008) in one of its reports stressed 'the importance of plugging [Singapore] into the international landscape to overcome both resource and market constraints' (25). Building on its geographical locale between the East and the West, English-speaking citizenry, and multiple connections in the region, the Council aspired to position Singapore 'as the world's cultural gateway to Asian arts and culture'. In this pursuit of a new competitive brand identity for Singapore, heritage was recognized by the country as a 'key ingredient in defining a vibrant and cosmopolitan global city' in the face of 'heightened competition amongst the world's cities' (NHB, 2008: 9).

However, Singapore's urban design does not necessarily seek to celebrate 'a deep cosmopolitanism' in its heritage presentation. According to Goh (2013), the heritage spaces in the city serve two functions; first, 'selling' the city to expatriate elites and global tourists who want to experience Asia; and second, producing a multicultural disciplined citizenry by domesticating differences. For example, the famous Little India community in the city centre has been redesigned for global consumption and is strategically separated from new migrant workers from India, who would reside in the city's outskirts. In this way, the urban racial and cultural diversity is tamed by gentrification and modernization of cultural heritage spaces, which inevitably results in the process of urban cultural amnesia (Deng, 2020). In this context, the SMP is one of Singapore's 'cultural products with a local flavor that remain steadfastly and safely within the mainstream tastes of global tourists' (Chong, 2005: 565).

In analysing the logic of the SMP's memory campaign, it is possible to differentiate across two basic international marketing strategies. On the one hand, the portal aims to engage a global viewer with memories collected to expose Singapore as a global place for cultural consumption. For instance, the campaign 'irememberStyle' features the celebratory collection of Club 21's, Asia's 'leading purveyor of luxury fashion' with retail extending over 250 global brands across nearly 400 stores in Asia (Club 21, n.d.). Likewise, the 'IrememberPlay' campaign aims to showcase world-famous television programming, motion pictures, and video games which at some point became a part of the informational reality of Singaporeans. It includes references to such media products as Transformers, Littlest Pet Shop, Nerf, PlaySkool or My Little Pony, among other globally beloved brands. A campaign promoted on the SMP in 2020, the 'DFS: A Chapter of Wonder Memories', driven by the world traveller's luxury retailer DFS and Changi Airport, does not leave any doubts about the strategic positioning of the portal as a virtual landing platform to sell the 'wonders' of Singapore to global consumers. All these memory campaigns perfectly situate the city within global retail chains and franchises, expanding its geographical horizons to international markets.

On the other hand, the SMP's campaign collections strike the viewer with the absence of focused space and little effort to feature or celebrate the different cultures that comprise Singaporean society. While Chinese citizens have always dominated, steadily making up almost 76 per cent of the total population for many decades (SS, 2020), the Government has put a lot of effort into the reproduction of the CMIO (Chinese, Malay, Indian, and Others) mythology, aiming to demonstrate a racially harmonious Singaporean society (Kathiravelu,

2017). For example, the first museum established in the country was the Asian Civilizations Museum, designed to showcase the cultural and historical backgrounds of the major ethnic groups in Singapore – Chinese, Malay, and Indians. This clearly illustrated the Singapore Government's priority to develop a national narrative of a city understood as the intermediary in Maritime Asia among diverse countries in the region and in international contexts (Heng and Aljunied, 2009).

As a heritage crowdsourcing portal, the SMP demonstrates a completely different social dynamic in terms of race representation. A quick search using the keyword 'Chinese' returns more than 72,000 memories, in comparison to 529 and 289 submissions that appear in response to the search of such keywords as 'Malay' and 'Indian' respectively. Furthermore, memory stories in Mandarin on the SMP constitute approximately 20 per cent of all submissions to the portal, while texts in Malay are very few, with no submissions in Bengali at all. In fact, there are no campaigns that would preserve the public memory of Indian or Malay cultures in Singapore, either mapping their dedicated urban communities like Little India, Arab Street, and Kampong Glam, or showcasing the cultural and religious holidays like Hari Raya, the major celebration in all Muslim cultures or Diwali, the festival of light celebrated by Hindus, Jains, Sikhs, and some Buddhists. The emphasis on Chinese culture, though, is evident through such campaigns as 'irememberChinatown', 'iremember ChineseNewYear', or 'irememberChingay', the famous Chinese Lunar New Year Street parade.

The SMP's representation of Singaporean culture perfectly reflects several decades of cultural and educational policies in the country that have carefully nurtured 'the Census quadratomy of CMIO (Chinese, Malay, Indian, and Others)' as 'building blocks of the Singapore nation', where Chinese elitism and cultural values always inevitably dominated and set the rules of the game (Barr and Skrbiš 2011: 51). While on a rhetorical level, the Singapore Government promotes its unique multiculturalism, secularism, and meritocracy based on national unity without compromising ethnic, religious, and cultural heritage or beliefs (Public Service Division, n.d.), since the early 1980s, the state system of multiracialism has served two key purposes. First, placating 'the minority races so that they accept a subordinate place in society and thus ensure social peace and order'. Second, 'inviting, cajoling and pressuring the minority races to actively embrace the supposed "values" of the dominant Chinese' (Barr and Skrbiš 2011: 252).

Memory campaigns such as 'The Singapore Story: My Heart, My Hope, My Home', 'Hands that brought us up', or 'The Greatest Gift of a Generation' would, of course, contain submissions that expose contributors' cultural and religious backgrounds and tell personal stories about Indian, Malay, and other cultures. However, these memories are strategically framed and amalgamated in pre-designed collections-containers under labels that instead portray Singapore as an 'imagined unified community'. Such framing allows the SMP to manage the cultural diversity of public contributions in such a way that they correspond to the Government objectives to construct, nurture, and celebrate the 'common national identity that must take precedence over our ethnic or religious identities' (PSD, n.d.). This strategic management and moderation of memory collection processes within the project turns the public crowdsourcing portal into a governmental tool of social control. The SMP 'canonizes', 'conserves', and makes a historical imprint out of living public memory, taking form in digital cultural products like photographs, video, or text contributions. In this way, a live public narrative or social memory, in Adorno's terms (1982) is being 'killed' or framed in a digital heritage collection. In other words, the born digital artefacts solicited through public contributions are being displaced from their original social communication environments and put into the new context of the online heritage archive to evoke feelings of national pride and 'a sense of place, community, belonging and opportunity'. As the section demonstrates, these social engineering strategies work well for both the nation-building and nation-branding ambitions of Singapore.

Conclusion

At the time of writing, while the SMP is still accessible online, the NLB shared that 'the current SMP portal has stopped accepting new submissions since 11 Jan 2023', because they are planning to reconceptualize the project in the future (NLB, 2023). They also indicated that it has been a 'successful campaign with more than a million memories contributed and preserved' to 'document Singapore national and socio-cultural history'. While the NLB does plan to revamp the crowdsourcing platform later in 2023, the closure of the portal, for now, signals that its 'success' as a virtual heritage space for citizens to preserve their memories is questionable. The problem with this digital heritage aggregator is that, in the hands of the Government, it turned into an ideological tool to achieve its geopolitical objectives, in terms of both legitimizing Singapore's history as a nation and positioning the country as an appealing regional cultural hub and a 'gateway to Asia' for tourism and consumption. This social engineering technology of public memory production could be better understood in terms of 'pseudo-participative interactivity' (Stiegler, 2010: 175). Framed and promoted as a genuine citizens' effort of self-representation, the portal in fact only created a frame of democratic participation without a real distribution of power. Political marketing exercised on behalf of the NLB, via numerous memory campaigns, turned the SMP portal into a simulacrum of national community representation for both local and global audiences.

'An important exercise for Singaporeans to reflect about documenting personal and institutional histories' (NLB, 2023), the SMP became a manipulative 'empty ritual' of participation 'despite rhetorical calls for a more active citizenry from above and below' (Cheng, 2018: 67). As a result, the majority of SMP public memories are 'of low quality and low relevance to Singapore's Urban Heritage', pointing at the audiences' 'mindless cognitive state' (Widodo et al., 2017: 329). It is also evident in empty comments sections on the portal, which failed to invite contributors for dialogue and deliberation, as SMP users simply refrained from participating in online conversations. The NLB (2023) indicated that 'memories contributed in the current SMP will be *selected* and preserved', as well as 'made accessible to the public progressively in the next three to four years'. These statements confirm that the portal is still being heavily curated, even in the transition from a temporary closure to a future preservation stage in which some memories will be removed as 'some items may not fall under [NLB] collection guidelines and will not be preserved' (NLB, 2023). Such arrangements convincingly demonstrate that the heritage aggregation as a public exercise to preserve the memories was and still is a highly controlled social engineering campaign for nation-building and nation-branding, rather than a public space for memory sharing and preservation.

The project became a perfect state virtual enlargement tool for the Government to pursue two objectives. On the one hand, it aimed to 'naturalize' public cultural memories and ambitions of the artificially created nation to promote an 'ideal Singapore society in the twenty-first century' (S21C, 2001). On the other hand, SMP strived to shape the country's image in the global arena as an appealing destination to indulge in modern culture. By rebranding its cultural image as a democratic innovative regional hub, 'where East meets the West', the SMP perfectly reflected the state's aspiration to position itself as a traditional Asian yet cutting-edge and technological society. While a decade ago, with the rise of web 2.0 hype and the rapid development of social media technologies, the SMP did bring regional and even international attention to the NLB's efforts to collect and document heritage, right now it looks like an outdated resource. This obsolescence manifests not so much in terms of the portal, design, functionality, or capabilities, which did not progress to meet the demands of contemporary netizens, but rather in terms of social relevance, as well as the cultural and historical value of its content to Singapore residents and visitors.

3 Building National Heritage Infrastructure: Trove

Introduction

Trove is an aggregator hosted by the National Library of Australia (NLA), which provides online access to six billion cultural heritage items from around 900 Australian collecting institutions (NLA, 2021). It aggregates metadata from collections sources and makes them searchable through a single interface online (https://trove.nla.gov.au/). Trove came about as part of the re-thinking of physical and digital spaces at the NLA in 2008 (Ayres, 2018). The recognition of siloes between format types, such as maps and books, and the desire to bring together information resources that were geographically distant from users and one another drove the original planning behind the project. The primary aim of Trove, to link up users with searched-for items, was facilitated by building on top of existing systems, specifically the Australian Bibliographic Network, a national database launched in 1981. This history of collaboration over geographical distance in Australia is notable and has been a definitive feature of Trove's service (Sherratt, 2016). In 2009 the Library released the first public version of Trove, in line with its strategic objective, to 'improve the delivery of information resources to the Australian public' (National Library of Australia, 2009). The interface was made up of interconnected systems to harvest, manage, index and deliver digital content. This section shows how the national framing of Trove is subject to different influences and political forces. The tensions between distinct digital heritage cultures of 'the Australian people' (NLA, 2022) will be the focus of analysis, allowing for examination of the geopolitics arising from Australia's contested national story.

Australian Geopolitics

Australia is an island-continent and nation which straddles the divide between its history and its geography. Its history as a former British colony has shaped the country's culture, language, and strategic partnerships. The colonization of Australia in 1788 was accompanied by violent conflicts and the displacement of First Nations Australians from their land, leading to a vast reduction in the Indigenous population by 1900 (Miller et al., 2012). British control over Australian territory subsequently influenced its governance, initially as part of the British Empire (1788–1850), then later as a member of the Commonwealth of Nations (1901 onwards). Australia gained legislative autonomy from Britain in 1942 and full legal independence in 1986. Yet it has retained close links with the UK and cooperation across a range of domains, including foreign policy, defence, security, trade, and economics (DFAT, 2022a).

At the same time, Australia's location in the Asia-Pacific region has meant that, since attaining independence, it has sought a diversification of alliances, both regionally and internationally (Flint, 2022). Since the 1950s, Australia has forged economic and strategic partnerships with Japan, and China is currently the country's largest trading partner (DFAT, 2022b). Also important is Australia's relationship with the United States and security treaties such as ANZUS (1951), which have had a defining role in its defence and foreign policy (Albinski and Tow, 2002). The more recent AUKUS pact with both the United States and the UK (The White House, 2021) further complicates Australia's position and standing with its neighbours. From a geopolitical perspective, it has been interpreted as a move towards stronger bilateral relations with the United States, and as part of a security strategy for the containment of China (Medcalf, 2020).

Australia's comparative isolation from the imperial rivalries and grand strategies associated with classical geopolitics has led some scholars to emphasize geographical distance as an explanatory factor for its semi-peripheral status in international affairs (Bogais et al., 2022). During the last twenty years, following China's economic ascendance, the notion of distance from Western powers assumes less significance than it may have done previously. However, it does indicate a partial rationale for Australia's divided position between Anglo military alliances and regional markets. This mixture of influences and alliances also plays out in the realm of culture. Ang et al. observe that 'Australian cultural diplomacy today has a strong regional focus' and there is political and policy consensus that 'it is in the country's national interest to establish closer links with the countries in the geopolitical region it finds itself in' (2015: 369). The attendant concept of soft power, originally understood as the ability to co-opt rather than coerce and set the political agenda in a way that shapes the preferences of others (Nye, 1990), has become popular in the context of Australia's cultural diplomacy discourse (Ang et al., 2015). Here, soft power is taken to be an appealing projection of the country's national culture abroad (Australian Government, 2012; Grincheva, 2019). In addition, the Australian Library and Information Association (ALIA) has suggested that regional relationships between galleries, libraries, archives, and museums (GLAMs) may strengthen political bonds and cultural understanding (ALIA, 2018). Digital platforms have been identified as a means of facilitating reciprocal cultural exchanges across GLAMs (Grincheva, 2020).

At the national level, institutions like the NLA have a mandate to collect and preserve documentary resources that are first and foremost connected to 'Australia and the Australian people' (NLA, 2022: 13). In terms of documentary heritage material, this has historically privileged the Anglophone culture that is the legacy of colonization. The NLA has been recognized as having a comparatively expansive idea of the Australian people (Neumann, 2019) and its activities have increasingly been oriented towards building collections that represent the Indigenous histories and heritage of Australia (NLA, 2022). The violent erasure of First Nations Australians from historical narratives makes this task of representation a contested question (Curthoys, 1999), one that is deeply interwoven into the national culture. The rest of the section unpacks these issues in relation to the Trove aggregator, which is managed by the NLA, and has been described as an example of soft power influence through digital access (Bell, 2022).

Trove: From 'Find and Get' to National Heritage Infrastructure

In her study of discourse in the NLA's policy documents, Emilia Bell (2022) argues that the construction and preservation of national identity is a key theme through which the institution engages with soft power. This soft power influence is located in the values and culture attached to national identity, through which overseas partnerships and collaborations can be promoted (Nye, 1999). As a digital service providing access to national heritage collections, Trove is viewed as a channel for mediating contact between Australia's national interests and its regional and international relationships (ALIA, 2018). Likewise, in the NLA's 2021–22 Annual Report, the centrality of Trove is acknowledged as a recognized brand and 'an essential part of Australia's cultural and research infrastructure' (2022: 35). This designation has emerged for Trove in the wake of its popular uptake and the role it has come to play in collaborative partnerships with other Australian GLAMs. Before considering Trove's impact, the discussion will first give some background to the development of the system and how it works.

Trove brought together a number of services that had previously been separate including Picture Australia, Music Australia, the Pandora Web Archive, and Australian Newspapers. It was designed to work through the aggregation of bibliographic, subject, and authority records metadata, meaning that it can surface and point to non-digital as well as digital resources. This functionality chimed with the ethos of 'find and get', which was a guiding principle for the early developers of Trove. The idea was intended to reduce dead ends in the system, so that even if a digital text or a physical item was unavailable, there would be pointers for how to obtain it. After its initial launch in 2009, there were new releases of Trove almost once a month, based on feedback from users, which contributed to the perception of Trove as a user-oriented service (Holley, 2011).

The front-end of Trove operates on a search-based model and has additional functionality which organizes results according to nine categories. These have been devised based on format type, but items can also appear in multiple categories (e.g. an illustrated book could be found in both books and images). This kind of deep searching is aided by Trove's indexing mechanisms; the service indexes its own database, fulltext content from the newspapers, archived websites, as well as fulltext content from books, journals and finding aids. A separate system indexes identity records for people and organizations, so that biographical or place information drawn from different contributors and associated resources can be grouped together in a record (Trove Website, 2022a). Therefore, Trove makes it possible to begin to forge connections between content that go beyond basic description and collections information.

Trove is distinctive because it both aggregates collections data and delivers digital content, including a substantial volume of digitized fulltext newspapers. The application of OCR and text searching to the newspapers has facilitated tools of social engagement such as crowdsourced text correction. Researchers comprise another user group, with many academics using the data made available through Trove's API to carry out new forms of large-scale analysis (Sherratt, 2016). These tools have cemented Trove's reputation as a collaborative venture, both with the partners it harvests data from and with users. They also contribute to the popularity of the service with the website receiving over 60,000 daily visits (NLA, 2021). While the majority of users are based in Australia, evaluation of Trove's website showed that 40 per cent of visitors access the service from locations overseas, making Trove a digital first point of contact with Australian heritage material (Ayres, 2013). It is also a knowledge base for Anglophone text sources internationally. A 2018 study revealed the wider impact of the NLA and Trove, listing their site among the top fifteen for external citations in the English-language version of Wikipedia (Wikimedia, 2022).

Trove's combination of national and international reach has been an element of its success and this has afforded it a more prominent position in the NLA's strategic planning. The institution attempts to balance its domestic and regional priorities in a range of areas. For example, in its Collection Development Policy, both Australian material and overseas material from the Asia-Pacific region are highlighted, though not to the same extent (NLA, 2020a: 34). These priorities are not necessarily incompatible; rather, building a rich national collection becomes a soft power resource for the promotion of cultural understanding abroad (Ang et al., 2015; Aukia, 2019; Bell, 2022). Furthermore, legacies of migration mean that the heritage of Australia and that of other regional cultures increasingly overlap. The NLA's new acquisitions for 2021–2022 include issues of the *Australian Chinese Weekly* and the *Australian Chinese Daily*, the largest Chinese-language newspapers in Australia (NLA, 2022: 22). Trove also makes selected Chinese Australian material available as part of its digitized newspaper collection (Sherratt, 2019). This emphasis on Chinese-language material is in-keeping with a long history of Chinese immigration to Australia, which continues to this day (DHA, 2022). It also reflects Government consensus that it is in Australia's national interests to forge closer links with China. The 2012 White Paper, *Australia in the Asian Century*, stressed China's growing economic power and recommended supporting Chinese participation in the region's strategic, political, and economic development (Australian Government, 2012).

However, broader geopolitical shifts, informed by Australia's security pacts with the United States, have started to throw the country's project of regional diplomacy into doubt. The Government's more wary security stance towards countries like China compounds longer-term issues around the lack of funding for diplomatic programmes (Ang et al., 2015). This ambivalence has started to surface in the NLA's collecting policies as well. The Library announced that in the period leading up 2030 'overseas collecting, including from Asia, will reduce' (NLA Website, 2022). The turn inwards to focus on domestic cultural collections has attracted criticism from some scholars. Writing in *The Canberra Times*, Edward Aspinall argued that 'Understanding Australia requires that we understand our Asian context. This is the approach that has guided the library in the past' (2020). The suggestion is that, while promoting stronger ties with Asia at the level of policy rhetoric, the Government has been unwilling to commit the resources needed to make it a reality.

Funding is also a factor that has shaped the development of Trove over the years. Despite its success, the service has been subject to different policies and pressures. In 2016, its future was threatened due to cuts in the NLA's budget. In response to a campaign to save Trove, the Government's Public Service Modernisation funding provided a one-off payment of $16.4 million over four years to bring it up to date (DITRDCA, 2020). The current Annual Report continues to underline the establishment of a sustainable funding model as an issue, and this landscape has influenced how collaboration with partners has evolved over the years (NLA, 2022: 3). Proposals for strengthening Trove's brand have been geared towards embedding partner organizations into the site, and this was a key feature of its redesign in 2020 (Walker, 2017). Moreover, in 2018 the NLA introduced a pricing model for partners to cover the costs of aggregating their digital content in Trove (NLA, 2020b: 34). This transitional pricing arrangement was updated in 2022. The logic behind these changes relates to a growing recognition of Trove as part of a national digital infrastructure (NLA 2021: 35). The current Strategy (2021) foregrounds this role for the service, as well as the relevance of its brand as an online portal into the documentary heritage of Australia.

The next section will consider how different digital heritage cultures surface in Trove and their geopolitical implications. The term 'digital heritage' is used in reference to material delivered or harvested by Trove's system; that is, digital heritage is understood to be bound up with information infrastructures and emergent in the tools used for search and discovery (Verhoeven, 2016).

Digital Heritage of the Nation

As the foregoing discussion shows, in its focus on 'collecting Australia', Trove walks a line between consolidating material for its domestic user base and the promotion of its national culture regionally and internationally. These different avenues for digital engagement involve distinct audiences. In its Strategy (2021), it is clear that Trove's primary audience is users based in Australia, and the NLA's strategic emphasis is on representing Australians in all their diversity (2022: 15). Trove's community of regular users comprises a significant component of the Australian user group, and they have a dedicated landing page on the current version of the site. These users are distinguished by the nature of their engagement with Trove as active participants through activities like text correction, transcription, tagging and indexing. The majority of users undertaking text correction are older or identify as retired (Ayres, 2013; Brew, 2019). This data suggests that the audience with the most direct engagement with Trove is narrower than might be hoped for, raising questions about how far crowdsourcing and interactive engagement can expand Trove's users to be more representative and inclusive of the Australian people. The kinds of initiatives that users have been invited to participate in may also partly explain this lack of diversity. Australia's national story has, at times, made it difficult to reconcile competing heritage narratives about its colonial past. A project that brings these issues into sharp relief is Click and Flick, a partnership between the NLA and Flickr, which sought to enable social photo-sharing from users (Hooton, 2006). The rationale for the project and the legacy of its archive in Trove warrants deeper consideration of the limits of digital engagement in promoting inclusion.

Click and Flick was a relatively early instance of a cultural heritage institution crowdsourcing social photography collections, whereby thematic groups were created on the NLA's Flickr account for members of the public to upload and tag their images. A well-publicized version of this method was the Great War Archive's Community Collection Model, a Flickr group dedicated to sharing people's stories and memorabilia from the First World War (Edwards, 2010). In the Click and Flick project, two groups – Australia Day and People, Places and Events – were set up on Flickr in January 2006. Metadata and thumbnail images from the groups were harvested on a weekly basis into the NLA's aggregator PictureAustralia, a forerunner of Trove. The motivation for the project was to 'build a diverse collection of images of national significance produced by individual Australians' (Hooton, 2007). These aims were met insofar as the project vastly expanded the contemporary image collection of PictureAustralia. Yet the creation of an Australia Day photo-sharing group immediately constrained the possibilities for diverse collections because of the holiday's controversial status. As the official national day of Australia, it marks the landing of the first British fleet in New South Wales in 1788. However, this event also marks the start of a violent period for the Indigenous inhabitants of the land and the start of colonization. The choice of the group theme was explained due to the launch date of Click and Flick being around the same time as Australia Day in January, thus serving as promotion for the project and providing an initial scope for collecting. After the first year of the project, over 12,000 contemporary images had been harvested by PictureAustralia from the two Flickr groups (Hooton, 2007). The subject matter of Australia Day images tended to feature celebrations of the national holiday between families and friends with photos including the national flag appearing prominently.

The promotion and uptake of the project was quite short-lived (2006–2008), and the Australia Day group was ultimately closed with all the images being transferred to People, Places and Events (flickr, 2022). However, photos did continue to be harvested by PictureAustralia and subsequently by Trove. These images are discoverable on Trove at the time of writing, and the Flickr account is still relatively active, with regular uploads of images from users. The Australia Day photos now sit among a much wider thematic group, but their aggregation in Trove also confers on them a disproportionate weight as an expression of national heritage culture. In inviting these contributions, Click and Flick was arguably facilitating a selective presentation of Australia's national story, failing to take account of the ways in which the date is contested and the erasure of the much longer history of First Nations people. For example, the project did not give as much exposure to Invasion Day Rallies, protests that have been held concurrently with Australia Day, since its establishment in 1938 (Pearson, 2017). This narrow portrayal of national heritage chimes with Stuart Hall's critique that 'A shared national identity depends on the cultural meanings which bind each member individually into the larger national story [...] It follows that those who cannot see themselves reflected in its mirror cannot properly "belong"' (1999: 4).

It is interesting to note the liminal status of the Flickr Australia Day images in Trove. While they were harvested by the aggregator and are discoverable on the website, they have not been accessioned by the NLA, meaning they are not in the official collections or subject to the institutional standards for image description. Without context or consistent descriptions, the extent to which the photos can be rendered meaningful is uncertain. They may retain meaning for the individuals who submitted them but their social history value is questionable. A lack of context for the images also plays out in relation to Trove's interface, which operates via a search bar on the landing page. If the Australia Day images appeared in a search results list, they would be difficult to trace back to the original Click and Flick project and the specific circumstances in which collecting took place. As Tim Sherratt observes, 'There will always be priorities in digitisation programs. There will always be short-term funding opportunities related to specific initiatives or events [. . .] these biases and distortions are not obvious to someone typing queries into a search box' (2016).

The Click and Flick case study demonstrates some of the tensions inherent in the heritage of English-speaking Australia as a settler colony. The contentious choice of Australia Day as a focal point for the project calls attention to the ethics of selection in digital heritage projects and the need to interrogate the shaping of the historical record (Christen et al., 2018; Evans and Wilson, 2018). The final part of the section turns to the complex relationship between the practice of digital heritage aggregation and the representation of Indigenous heritage. Here, the idea of heritage based on the founding of Australia as a modern nation-state is met with the challenge of sovereignty claims by First Nations Australians, which have been characterized as an expression of Indigenous geopolitics (Gibson, 2016).

Indigenous Digital Heritage Cultures

From the period 2016–2020, the NLA began a project to update Trove, following its grant from the Government's Modernisation Fund. The aim was to redesign the front end of the service, making it more accessible and easier to navigate, which culminated in a relaunch in 2020 (Brew, 2020). The NLA's strategic focus on diverse communities and presenting stories in a culturally appropriate way informed the project and this was evident in how the heritage of First Nations Australians was foregrounded in the new website. The upgraded Trove includes the addition of cultural warnings for sensitive records, the ability for users to report culturally sensitive material, and a First Australians landing page. The NLA has also added Austlang codes to relevant item records, allowing searches for content in Aboriginal and Torres Strait Islander languages

(Trove Website, 2022b). Several of these features were added based on feedback from user consultations that Trove was not always culturally safe, with some images and descriptions requiring additional warnings or restrictions (Brew, 2019). Trove's drive to be more inclusive has been described as a collaboration involving 'partners, and ongoing discussions with First Australian peoples' (Trove Website, 2022b). This emphasis on working in partnership reflects a shift towards people-centred practices in libraries and archives, specifically as they relate to community and social justice movements (Flinn et al., 2009; Cook, 2013; Caswell et al., 2018).

Trove's remit is to make its content 'freely accessible' (2021) but, in dealing with Indigenous heritage, it must comply with communities' local and specific conditions for circulating material, much of which cannot be shared publicly. Deidre Brown and George Nicholas point out that 'Indigenous peoples are concerned that culturally significant aspects of their heritage have often been appropriated or made into commodities, or used in inappropriate ways [. . .] This is not to imply that open access is bad, but to point out that there are uses of other people's heritage that may be inappropriate or unappreciated' (2012: 309). A large portion of the Indigenous heritage content in Trove comes from the Australian Institute of Aboriginal and Torres Strait Islander Studies (AIATSIS). Founded in 1964, the Institute is also a Government organization and is internationally recognized for its ethical practice (AIATSIS Website, 2022). The nature of AIATSIS' collections means that it cannot provide public access to all the items it holds and material is restricted according to Indigenous community protocols. Aggregated metadata about items is searchable and viewable in Trove, rather than digitized images of the items themselves. A senior archive officer at AIATSIS remarked that being included in Trove was aligned with their mission to make collections more accessible and interoperable with those of the NLA (Wood, 2018).

As part of Trove's upgrade, efforts to respect the cultural sensitivities around Indigenous heritage have been quite extensive. The NLA's latest Annual Report demonstrates an awareness of the need to ensure its national collection holds material of importance to Indigenous Australia (2022: 15). From the perspective of the NLA, being representative of the nation entails diversifying the historical record and working with Indigenous communities to achieve this. Because it is a large, federated state, the question of diverse representation also applies to the cultural politics of each of Australia's states and territories. Heritage management can be subject to variations in provincial (state) legislation (Johnston, 2021), which gives rise to specific kinds of struggles for recognition by those who are the original custodians of the land. The national collecting framework obscures the complex dimensions of identity, place, and history in which these struggles are formed and risks homogenizing different Indigenous heritage cultures.

In addition to the issue of cultural homogenization, Australia's colonial history means that national and government institutions are not always considered to be appropriate or safe environments for the protection of Indigenous heritage. A US-based research study into national digital strategies found that community archives often 'strive to maintain autonomy over and control access to digitized materials in their care in line with the particular values and protocols of the communities they represent and serve' (Caswell et al., 2017). In the case of First Nations people, the issue of autonomy is central: many communities have a strong desire to retain the rights to their collections and histories, and exercise extreme caution regarding relationships with national institutions (Dallwitz et al., 2019). The idea of Indigenous heritage itself also holds a distinctive set of values and meanings. An aggregator like Trove has been designed as an information discovery tool for predominantly documentary heritage. The significance of stories and living heritage in Indigenous cultures cannot be easily reconciled with this kind of system. Margo Neale explains that 'Archives exist in places other than books, documents stored and other modern formats [. . .] In the ur-archive humans are documents, archived according to kin and ancestral relations' (2017: 269). Aggregation, a process largely based on drawing together item records, is consequently limited in its capacity to accommodate knowledge systems that are indexed in relationships to ancestors and country.

That is not to say that digital methods are incompatible with the needs of Indigenous communities. In Australia, there are a number of projects which have been developed collaboratively, to create culturally appropriate controls over access to heritage. These kinds of projects respond to the challenge that not all forms of heritage lend themselves to being searchable and publicly available online. Aṟa Irititja and the Keeping Culture knowledge management system is one example of this approach. It is a project and archive for Ngaanyatjarra, Pitjantjatjara and Yankunytjatjara people (Aṉangu). Originally instigated by the Aṉangu, Aṟa Irititja, meaning 'stories from a long time ago', has grown from a filemaker database on a mac, to a web application capable of making highly referenced databases. Following the wishes of the community, the software has been specifically designed to showcase stories and links between entities such as people, places and events, in line with Aṉangu cultural requirements (Mann, 2018). As regards autonomy, the perspective of those involved in the project is that:

> The Ar̲a Irititja Project has always been a fiercely-independent, community facing organisation [. . .] the project does not consider itself obliged to provide non-Anangu researchers with access to its collections. Nevertheless, research that is approved, based on community consultation, and carried out with due sensitivity is welcomed and supported. (Dallwitz et al., 2019)

Douglas Mann (2018), who developed the Keeping Culture knowledge system, expressed a similar view that what the community wants and what is helpful as a tool are key drivers for his work. He was also positive about the potential of technology to structure differentiated access to Indigenous heritage and questioned the idea that preserving culture should automatically mean sharing culture. As suggested, Trove's management by the NLA and its own priorities as a national collecting institution make access a condition of the service. These different motivations and audiences mean that it is not necessarily possible or desirable to construct a technical bridge between projects like Ar̲a Irititja and Trove. It is clear, however, that their existence contributes to a richer and more nuanced digital heritage environment. As Joanne Evans (2018) put it in a conversation about content management systems, 'The answer is never one, it's always many.'

In the geopolitical context, the contrast between a government project like the NLA's Trove and the community-driven Ar̲a Irititja could be compared to the shaping of Australia's national interests as a geopolitical actor versus the sovereign claims of First Nations people, which underpin global geopolitical relations, particularly with respect to land rights (Gibson, 2016). These tensions also correspond to distinct traditions of geopolitics; while the study of statecraft and patterns in global politics has been the mainstay of academic scholarship, the field of critical geopolitics has emerged to account for the politicization of place via geographical and spatial assumptions, and the process by which interests and identities come into being (Ó Tuathail, 1999; Dodds et al., 2016). In this vein, Chris Gibson has coined the term 'Indigenous geopolitics' as a means of drawing attention to First Nations people as agents of political change. He writes,

> Manifold engagements with indigenous peoples – in colonial encounters, in government policy, in the spaces of contemporary everyday life – have deeply shaped the world we now know. Examinations of indigenous peoples and geopolitics bring into sharp relief questions of land and control, resources and livelihoods, agency and cultural identity. (2016: 421)

Gibson goes on to suggest that First Nations claims for recognition in countries like Australia constitute a geopolitics from below, by presenting a challenge to the legitimacy of colonial settlement (2016; see also Coe, 1994). Furthermore, demands for land rights, resources, and self-governance destabilize the myth of an Australian nation that is founded on the pioneering spirit of white settlers (Byrne, 1996; Curthoys, 1999). Such demands, which form part of what could be described as an Indigenous geopolitical agenda, operate beyond national borders, with some communities seeking to build links among First Nations people in other places. In its rejection of the logic of Western nation-states, Indigenous geopolitics is a domain of activism and practice that offers alternative political possibilities. Yet, at the same time, Indigenous groups face the constant curtailment of their self-determination efforts, due to government strategies of containment (Gibson, 1999). One battleground where these struggles play out is in the realm of heritage, both in terms of contested histories and in what has been called 'the persistent colonial topography of knowledge production' (Gibson, 2016: 432), a reference to the dominance of Anglophone scholarship and the structuring of knowledge according to Western values. This point connects to the inquiry into Trove and its aggregation function. Large-scale aggregators' drive towards standardization and information discovery reflect the aspirations of universal knowledge, to organize and classify the world. Decolonial writers have highlighted the historical and geographical specificity of universalism and its role in the consolidation of European colonial power (Shiva, 1993; Mignolo, 2002). These insights are important for establishing the partiality of universal knowledge and the constraints of aggregation as a knowledge infrastructure.

The independence of the Ar̲a Irititja project can therefore be seen in light of wider Indigenous movements for self-determination and a geopolitical outlook that is both locally situated and globally relevant. This positioning also clarifies the reasons for non-participation in government-affiliated or nationally framed projects. While cultural safety and care for Indigenous heritage are paramount, it also represents a deliberate separation from the logic of the nation and its technical apparatus, which has been responsible for the displacement of Indigenous knowledge practices.

Conclusion

Since its launch over a decade ago, Trove has developed from a discovery tool (Holley, 2011) to a principal player in Australia's digital heritage infrastructure (NLA, 2022). The number of GLAMs that contribute content continues to grow and it is Trove's mission to further diversify its heritage partners in order to establish it as 'Australia's sovereign cultural resource' (NLA, 2021: 14). In broader terms, Trove's management by the NLA makes it representative of national collecting interests and subject to the Australian Government's cultural agenda. This agenda is motivated by geopolitical goals. Australia has sought to build strong connections in the Asia-Pacific region, with a view to improving cultural relations and facilitating economic and social gains (Australian Government, 2012). On the other hand, at the domestic level, the Government is increasingly bringing to the fore First Nations heritage. In its 2023 Cultural Policy, one of the strategic objectives is to 'support the telling of First Nations histories and stories in Australia's galleries, libraries, archives and museums' (DITRDCA, 2023: 22). The NLA's Annual Report states a similar priority to strengthen 'partnerships with Indigenous communities and deliver culturally appropriate programs and services' (2022: 26). Trove's upgrade has taken steps towards this but, as the section has shown, Australia's colonial history makes the task of representing Indigenous heritage a difficult and contradictory one. That does not mean that the NLA's efforts to create a more representative collection of the Australian people should not continue, but independent, community-based projects also require recognition and support.

Crucially, the case of Trove demonstrates that the technical workings of heritage aggregators are a political matter and have a bearing on much bigger debates around inclusion, community agency, national identity, and cultural governance. Aggregation is intimately linked to the technologies of knowledge underpinning modern nation-states. Given this fact, Trove's technical structure is also constitutive of it as a national expression of digital geopolitics. This section has revealed some limitations of digital heritage aggregation as a means of navigating the complex national story of Australia and the need for alternative heritage spaces and geopolitical frameworks.

4 Constructing Virtual Europe: Europeana

Introduction

The Europeana aggregator brings together cultural heritage data from around 4000 European galleries, libraries, museums, and archives (GLAMs) (Europeana, 2020) and is funded primarily through the European Commission (EC), the Executive Body of the European Union (EU). The origins of Europeana date back to 2005, when it was first envisaged as a European digital library. The project was motivated by the announcement of Google Books (originally called Google Print) in 2004–2005 (Jeanneney, 2007). Google planned to digitize and index books from a number of major US and UK library collections, initially those housed at the Universities of Michigan, Harvard, Stanford, Oxford, and the New York Public Library. Inspired by the lost library of Alexandria, the intention was to digitize and make available approximately fifteen million volumes within a decade (Auletta, 2010: 95). The EC's concern was that a US-based company would end up privatizing a large volume of European print works. In response, the proposal was made for an equivalent European programme that was open access, and digital libraries were announced as one of three flagship projects in the EC's i2010 Strategy (2005) (Europa, 2010). Jean-Noel Jeanneney, the former Director of the National Library of France, was a keen proponent of the digital library concept, asserting that 'many Europeans [...] refuse to accept that a cultural work might be considered and treated as just another piece of merchandise' (2007: 6). Jeanneney's ideas were taken up by the former President of France Jacques Chirac (1995–2007), who, in 2005, signed a joint letter with the leaders of Germany, Hungary, Italy, Poland, and Spain recommending the creation of a European digital library (Cousins, 2017). Support from other Member States and national libraries followed, and in 2007, the EC formally backed the proposal. Europeana's prototype aggregation database was unveiled in November of 2008. Starting with approximately 4.2 million items, that number has since risen to over 50 million, making Europeana one of the largest aggregators of cultural heritage data. This section explores the geopolitical imperatives of Europeana and how it operates within the wider context of the EU. The aim is to examine how these imperatives are imagined and applied in Europeana's policy and strategy documents and in its technical practice.

Geopolitics: Fostering Regional Cohesion

The EU represents a singular entity within international politics, especially in terms of the values upon which membership is conditional: democracy, rule of law, social justice, and respect for human rights (Manners, 2002). On that basis, Ian Manners and Thomas Diez call the EU a normative power, writing, 'the discourse of the EU as a normative power constructs a particular self of the EU [...], while it attempts to change others through the spread of particular norms' (2007: 174). The 'self' of the EU, it is implied, is grounded in those principles outlined earlier, while the spread of its norms is achieved through decision-making bodies like the EC and policies that have the normative identity of the EU at their core. Cultural heritage initiatives have been recognized as playing a key part in this process (Lähdesmäki, 2014). The EC's efforts to forge a shared European culture have been compared with the process of national identity-building, made famous by Eric Hobsbawm and Terence Ranger (1992) through the concept of invented tradition. Objects and practices, such as the founding of national archives and heritage, inform this process of 'ritualisation and formalisation' (Hobsbawm and Ranger, 1992: 4). If the rise of national consciousness is demonstrated by maintaining continuity with particular narratives of the past, it is also characterized by a tendency for nations to define themselves against others (Hall, 1992). Similarly, the EC's cultural projects are intimately linked to its goal of cementing and popularizing a cohesive European identity (Shore, 2006). The creation of the European flag, the European passport, and the Euro currency have all entailed the use of symbols that could be identified with invented tradition (Delanty, 1995; Macdonald, 2013).

The unifying bent of the EU has been more pronounced following the expansion of the cultural sector in the 1970s (Tretter, 2011), and has gained momentum since the Maastricht Treaty (1992), which adopted an article explicitly focusing on culture (Valtysson, 2018; Lähdesmäki et al., 2020). Shared European values and culture have also been promoted in programmes, including the European Capital of Culture, the European Heritage Label, and Creative Europe. These initiatives have been criticized because their representation of Europe is often based on a highly selective set of cultural influences and universal values (Passerini, 1998; Shore, 2000). Yet they only constitute part of the strategy by which the EC has sought to further transnational integration. Another long-standing cultural policy slogan is 'unity in diversity', a gesture towards cultural pluralism that also emphasizes the overarching unity of Europe. An article by Maryon McDonald (1996) suggests that this phrase had been in circulation for some time prior to the 1990s, although it was adopted as the official motto of the European Union in 2000 (Europa, 2022). In theory, it works by fostering European citizenship through cultural diversity in order to loosen national ties, a move which has been reflected in policy documents such as the New European Agenda for Culture. For example, one of the objectives of the Agenda is to harness 'the power of culture and cultural diversity for social cohesion' (Europa, 2018: 2). Here, the logic of unity in diversity requires that the former takes precedence over the latter and diversity is only encouraged to the extent that it does not obstruct unity.

Although this contradiction makes it difficult to appreciate the substance of the proposition beyond political rhetoric, anthropological research into the organizational structure of the EC indicates that such contradictions shed light on important aspects of the European project. Marc Abélès (2004) discerns a dimension of uncertainty in the working culture of the EC that he relates to the EU's initial principles of *engrenage* or 'action trap' for cooperation between member states; in agreeing on a specific course of action, member states would find themselves obliged to take another set of actions that pointed in a direction they had not necessarily intended to go. In line with the theory of *engrenage*, he argues that the underlying paradigm of the European political process is less one of unification than of harmonization and rationalization (2004: 23). These terms refer to a process that demands continual compromise and negotiation. The result is that European policy begins to influence national politics without spelling out its political goals; it is an indefinite process, the conclusion of which is never quite achieved. Abélès associates these features with a larger practice of Europe-building, one whereby Europe comes into being as 'a virtual object' (2004: 6).

The concept of virtual Europe corresponds with how the EC's policy, through slogans like unity in diversity, both feeds on and reproduces forms of identification and difference, and reflects the indefinite geographical and geopolitical status of the EU. Yet these same manoeuvres also constitute a mode of governing. In this scheme, cultural heritage is less about access to the past than entry to an indeterminate future. Abélès quotes one EC official as saying: 'At the Commission everything goes faster than in an ordinary administration. Everything goes forward, there is no going back. It's a little like if one drives without a rear-view mirror' (2004: 3). In an interview with the author, the former Chair of the Europeana Foundation Nick Poole made a similar comment about Europeana itself, suggesting that the initiative is in-keeping with the tone of the EC's cultural policy more broadly:

> I have come to regard Europeana chiefly as a process rather than a destination. The process is one both of asserting a European cultural identity [. . .] and of identifying where it is located so that people can discover and experience it. (Poole, 2014).

The repeated occurrence of words like 'identifying' and 'building' point towards a shared language and set of terms for the operations by which European integration might be achieved. This aim is tied to the geopolitical objectives of the EU, to act as a unified commercial power and improve the global competitiveness of the organization. Europeana can be seen as part of its early efforts to test and extend that power in the digital realm. Details of how this distributed database was developed present an opportunity for consideration of how the logic of harmonization was woven into the technical fabric of the project.

Building Europeana, 'Harmonizing' Cultural Collections

In the initial stages, it was decided that Europeana would not store digital objects on a central server, both because of cost implications and because some national libraries had already carried out large-scale digitization activities (Erway, 2009). Instead, it would function as an aggregator of metadata about existing digital objects and point to the institutional sites where they were held. Here, the broad term 'digital object' is understood to encompass a range of artefacts, including thumbnail images, digital photographs of artworks, and other visual material and digital scans of text and print works. The descriptive metadata for those digital objects facilitates their discovery online. The metadata feeds Europeana's distributed network database and makes the content accessible at https://www.europeana.eu/. In addition, all its metadata is licensed under the Creative Commons CC0 Public Domain Dedication (Europeana, 2014).

At the time of its launch, Europeana was focused on building up a large volume of digital content, consistent with its strategic objective of reaching thirty million items in 2015 (Europeana, 2011). By 2025, the plan was to cover 'all of Europe's digitized cultural heritage' (Europeana, 2011: 5). The Digital Libraries Initiative conveyed a similar view, which was furthered through the coordination of a High Level Expert Group on Digital Libraries in 2009. In a final report commissioned by the EC, the Group concluded that:

> Digitisation and online accessibility needs to be achieved in full respect of the current copyright rules, while for cultural institutions there is the need for copyright reform and further harmonisation at European level to create the appropriate conditions for large scale digitisation. (see Marton, 2011: 68)

This excerpt registers one of the greatest barriers to large-scale digitization, in the form of copyright restrictions. Such restrictions undoubtedly informed Europeana's focus on digital object metadata rather than digitization. Yet, it is notable that the problem of copyright is cast as one of harmonization, the suggestion being that greater cooperation between member states would contribute to solving it. Another report from that period contains the same word, but this time in relation to streamlining the legal deposit process for cultural heritage material to avoid the issue of duplicate copies across the EU (Lévy et al., 2011: 29).

A tendency towards harmonization can also be discerned in the European Data Model (EDM). Europeana put a lot of effort into the development of this resource description framework. It was designed as an integration medium for metadata sourced from different data providers, to then be harvested by the Europeana aggregator (Isaac, 2013). The point was to make data from disparate GLAM collections interoperable and cross-searchable. However, the EDM's interoperability principles mirrored the policy drive for greater European integration, especially because the process required datasets to comply with EDM requirements, in order to establish minimum compatibility with Europeana. These political dimensions of aggregation have seldom been owned in the project.

Europeana holds the metadata about digital objects featured in its collections, but the objects themselves are held in the databases of GLAM sites. They therefore retain the contextual information relevant to the collections from which they are drawn. Consequently, aspects of Europeana's presentation are influenced by the pre-existing collection structures of individual (national) organizations. Marija Dalbello observes this precedent for the arrangement of physical collections to be reproduced in digital projects. Writing of the cultural record that heritage institutions are concerned with maintaining, she argues that 'studying how digital libraries are involved in the production of knowledge is crucial to our understanding of how memory institutions are currently shaping this record in the digital environment' (2004: 267). She has also remarked on the way technological developments can become intertwined with existing cultural imperatives in institutional settings. Signs of this tendency can be found in some of her qualitative research into national libraries. Of the EC's digital culture programme, she quotes one interviewee as saying: 'I think libraries can go along with this policy [of a unified Europe], because we can cooperate, we always did that [. . .] I think that politics in Europe and what libraries would like to do is very near together' (2009: 39).

Cultural heritage institutions, then, not only provide a model for organizing content but a framework for institutional cooperation, in which their own sense of building political cohesion in Europe becomes explicit. As Alexander Badenoch suggests, 'The Europeanization of digital heritage (is) a project of technological harmonization' (2011: 299). The effects of these changes go beyond the aggregation process itself, and indicate a drive towards greater standardization. Viewed in this way, the duplication of terms like harmonization across the EC's technical and cultural policy seems more than coincidental. Harmonization is a form of governmental rationality (Foucault, 1991), whereby the EC creates the conditions for collaboration between institutions and governments, in order that they become more closely aligned. The idea of harmonization chimes with the logic of standardization, of rendering memorable, and thus governable, with the aim of acting on the present. The technical instantiation of these modes of acting in Europeana and its model for metadata also have implications for its building of a European heritage culture underpinned by the EU's normative interests and values. Via analysis of policy documents and current initiatives, the next section draws out how Europeana is a strategically constructed digital heritage space. It also considers how the geopolitical agenda of the EU has been inflected in Europeana, both as a supranational project of political cohesion (virtual Europe) and as a global economic power aspiring to digital sovereignty.

From Digital Library to Digital Sovereignty

Throughout its development, Europeana has been dominated by a vision of building and discovery, shifting from the concept of a digital library (2011–2015) to a digital ecosystem (2020–2025). The change in focus from a library portal to a networked platform and partnership organization is one way in which the project has measured its progress and relative success. The umbrella term Europeana is also indicative of a desire to go beyond associations with particular institutions. It currently encompasses a number of organizations, consisting of the core operator, the Europeana Foundation, in collaboration with the Europeana Aggregators' Forum and the Europeana Network Association (Europeana, 2020: 41).

The legacy of the digital library proposal was notable in Europeana's first Strategic Plan (2011–2015). The document announced that 'Europeana is assembling the most comprehensive, trustworthy and authoritative collection of Europe's cultural and scientific heritage ever compiled' (2011: 12). The role of GLAMs as cultural gatekeepers was also foregrounded, which helps to contextualize the centrality of the library as a metaphor and anchor point for the original thinking around the project. However, the view of European culture as an end in itself vied with the obligation to provide a means of engaging with the public, for example, in its ambition to create models which would 'allow Europeana to bring in user content without compromising our authoritative positioning and with appropriate levels of mediation' (Europeana, 2011: 19). Hence, user-generated content was encouraged but not so far as to compromise the 'authoritative positioning' of Europeana's collections, revealing a tension between user participation and the prioritization of trustworthy content (see also Valtysson, 2012).

From 2014, Europeana started to revise its purpose as a single access point to European culture. In its 2015–2020 Strategy, the section headed 'From Portal to Platform' acknowledged, 'We need to reconsider our initial aim of building a single access digital museum, library and archive for Europe – a place where you're invited to look back at the great achievements of the past [. . .] People want to re-use and play with the material, to interact with others and participate in creating something new' (Europeana, 2014: 10). Here, the conflict between the authoritative positioning of cultural institutions and user engagement moved towards the latter in line with Europeana's uptake of the platform model and the wider dominance of platform-based Internet services. Instead of endorsing the portal as a destination website, the platform was defined as 'a place not only to visit but also to build on, play in and create with' (Europeana, 2014: 10). The idea was to make the content easier to reuse or export, as well as feeding into other sites that users habitually use, like Wikipedia. The language of innovation and transformation in some ways continued the trope of building that was a feature of the first strategy. But Europeana was positioned as a component of the digital information environment, rather than a gatekeeper to knowledge.

Europeana 1914–1918 (www.europeana1914-1918.eu/en), a project for the First World War Centenary (2011–2017), put this new approach into practice. Using the Europeana database, online content was aggregated from national collections, in conjunction with several European roadshows, where people brought their manuscripts and memorabilia from the war to be digitized. In addition, there was an online collections form on the website, where personal stories and images could be uploaded. The intention was that, through a mixture of stories from the public, national collections, and film archives, the experiences of the First World War could be communicated from diverse perspectives, across Europe and the world. The project also brought to light different cultures of remembering the war, as when roadshows in Germany were better attended than those in the UK. One of the organizers, Alun Edwards, attributed this to the history of WWI being more strongly communicated in British public museums, in contrast with the personal family histories and objects associated with German experiences (see Dunin-Wąsowicz, 2015).

The scope of Europeana 1914–1918 involved a shift in priorities, from aggregation to curation. Europeana's original idea was that aggregating and making digital heritage content available would lead to higher engagement, and this was not the case. Nick Poole acknowledged that 'access as a principle has failed almost entirely because it is passive – we have had to learn to move on from passive provision of access to proactive engagement with audiences' (2014). Europeana 1914–1918 achieved that because it invited individual and collective worldwide contributions, looking at the broader impact of WWI beyond the institutional walls of GLAMs. The material was also available for reuse, allowing for adaptation of the content. The centenary of the war provided an opportunity for the exploration of different heritage cultures, while at the same time it was framed as a shared memory of pan-European catastrophe. It could therefore be argued that contributors to the 1914–1918 project became implicated in Europeana's transnational identity-building enterprise; through targeting different localities, potential actors, local institutions, and populations, down to individuals, Europeana marshalled a diversity of voices into an overarching narrative of WWI. This unifying narrative was arguably more significant in the period 2015–2016, when the project was live, because of emerging uncertainty occasioned by the UK referendum on EU membership, which voted in favour of withdrawing from the Union (Calligaro, 2021). Despite attempts to instrumentalize the shared history of the war, it remains uncertain whether enlisting users as active participants led to a closer identification with the specifically *European* heritage the project sought to promote. As Sharon Macdonald notes, the idea of the European past is more often experienced as 'a repertoire of (sometimes contradictory) tendencies and developments' (2013: 2).

Europeana 1914–1918 combined existing collections data with a greater emphasis on individual stories, representing a change in method, employed when previous efforts failed to engage audiences in anticipated ways. But the project was still focused on valorizing European identity, even while it foregrounded a diversity of memories and experiences of the war. This strategy had an orientation towards internal cohesion, in that it sought the cultivation of a virtual European public via participation in a shared heritage and history. However, Europeana's goal of shoring up transnational identity has not only been an inward member state-facing project, it has also been directed outwards. European integration forms part of the EU's broader geopolitical agenda, as evidenced by policy documents such as the 2016 Strategy for International Cultural Relations, which highlights an integrated approach to cultural heritage for Europe (EC, 2016: 11). In this context, Europeana can be viewed as both a tool of cultural diplomacy and a means of increasing the EU's global competitiveness in the digital economy. Of the political logic of Europeana, Nanna Bonde Thylstrup goes as far as to assert that the aggregator 'produces a new form of cultural memory politics that converge national and supranational imaginaries with global information infrastructures' (Bonde Thylstrup, 2018: 57). The point here is that the territorial process of delimiting Europe through cultural and symbolic initiatives sits alongside a growing reliance on networked infrastructures of connectivity, which operate beyond and between national and supranational structures.

Building digital infrastructure has recently come to occupy a central position in EU policy. Much discussion has coalesced around the idea of digital sovereignty, understood as the 'ability to act independently in the digital world', for example, in matters of data protection and compliance (Madiega, 2020). The main driver for the adoption of this concept can be attributed to concerns arising from the EU's dependence on non-EU technologies and platforms, and their attendant economic and social influence: what has been described as a perceived colonization of the EU digitally (Liaropoulos, 2021). Being digitally sovereign, then, is also about achieving the technological capacity to become independent from foreign companies. However, this entails acting in accordance with the EU's own normative principles and values, a more difficult task given the declining priority accorded to these values in contemporary international politics (Higgott, 2020). The EU's commitment to asserting itself as a normative power vies with its need to maintain multilateral cooperation with strategic partners. Daniel Fiott summarizes the situation as follows: ‘If it is accepted that the EU has dependencies in areas such as health, critical supplies, digital technologies, and security and defence, then there is a need to ensure that the EU can secure its interests in such a way as to strengthen the multilateral order and play a key role alongside core partners such as the United States’ (2021: 4). To address the technology gap and attempt to keep pace with global leaders like China and the United States, the EU has allocated nearly €80 billion to digital infrastructure development in major areas, including 5G, big data, cloud computing, and Artificial Intelligence (AI). Concurrently, EU policymakers have launched new programmes such as Digital Europe and the European Data Strategy, containing plans for the creation of European data spaces to leverage the potential of big data, while also giving EU-based companies and individuals increased control over their data (Madiega, 2020).

In Europeana’s latest 2020–2025 Strategy, the impact of debates about digital sovereignty can be read into its portrayal of itself as part of a larger ‘ecosystem’ and ‘European infrastructure’ (2020: 41). The importance of infrastructure began to emerge from 2015 onwards, when Europeana became one of the EC’s Digital Service Infrastructures (DSI), funded under the Connecting Europe Facility (CEF) (Europeana, 2020). The new Strategy brings this function to the fore. It explicitly references the Digital Europe Programme’s pledges, to empower the cultural heritage sector in its digital transformation, and identifies its number one priority as strengthening European cultural heritage infrastructure (Europeana, 2020: 27). Some related initiatives are geared towards providing better services for GLAMs as data providers and more efficient aggregation processes (Europeana, 2020: 28). To that end, Europeana has aligned itself with the EU’s data spaces, and in 2021 the EC published a recommendation locating Europeana at the heart of building a common European data space for cultural heritage (2021a: 5).

This terminology has also started to inform how Europeana staff describe the initiative; as Collections Engagement Manager Douglas McCarthy explained, ‘Europeana is really part of a wider digital public space and being accessible, findable and traceable are really core elements of our work’ (2022). At Europeana’s 2022 conference, sessions were focused on how Europeana could reinvent itself along the lines of becoming a data space, taking on more of a role as broker between national-level aggregators and commercial platforms interested in incorporating cultural heritage data (Europeana Conference, 2022). Becoming a data space also necessitates Europeana moving away from labour-intensive data standardization practices associated with the EDM; the Strategy acknowledges the need to introduce systems to help streamline metadata aggregation to allow for quicker updates to the website (Europeana, 2020: 28). Behind such statements is an awareness of Europeana's own reliance on cultural institutions to supply collections data and the need to enable ease of access and reuse of that data in the wider knowledge economy. By positioning itself as an advocate for cultural heritage data, Europeana is at once seeking to demonstrate its continued relevance to GLAMs in terms of collaboration, while also adopting a model that makes it more amenable to relationships with dominant commercial Internet platforms.

Concerning Europeana's collections, the new Strategy stresses the importance of establishing a common multilingual access point to digital European heritage and harnessing the potential of the website as a powerful platform for storytelling (Europeana, 2020: 17). Both themes pertain to how heritage is envisaged in the project, especially at a time when the idea of the EU is itself under intensifying strain due to a resurgence in national-populist movements across member states (Borriello and Brack, 2019). Enriching descriptive metadata and enabling search in different languages is a primary objective for Europeana. The dominance of relatively few languages in the database – over half of all the material is in English, German, Dutch, Norwegian, or French – makes the development of more diverse multilingual searching a pressing issue (Daley, 2021). The status of English as the lingua franca of the Internet partially accounts for this bias but there are political grounds for Europeana's drive to be more linguistically representative, such as the United Kingdom's exit from the EU in 2020. Currently, the Europeana website can be navigated in twenty-seven languages and the EDM enables object metadata to be enriched with multilingual values, so that relevant results can be surfaced regardless of the language used to perform a search (Daley, 2021).

In practice, though, this functionality largely rests on multilingual labels being added to the collections data supplied by GLAMs and other providers, meaning that search results can be somewhat uneven, depending on whether they have enriched metadata or not. Another issue is that, while it is possible to search the website in a range of languages, metadata for individual records does not change to the search language. Europeana plans to improve multilingual information discovery by using complementary processes of data enrichment such as machine translation (Europeana, 2020: 35). Europeana's multilingual chatbot is one example of this approach. Through discerning patterns and connections between aggregated collections data, the chatbot offers interactive scenarios for engaging with Europeana and is available in six languages (Culturebot website, 2022). Ostensibly, embedding multilingualism in Europeana can be understood as a reflection of the project's transnational values, but it also wants to establish itself as a data space and is motivated by the recognition that unlocking non-Anglophone data is fundamental to ensuring the long-term health and economic growth of the service (Parkinson, 2020).

The emphasis on storytelling in the 2020–2025 Strategy continues the push for curated content that was a feature of earlier projects like Europeana 1914–1918. This emphasis has been complemented by work carried out by the Europeana Network Foundation, such as that of the digital storytelling task force. The final report of the group envisions stories as a central pillar of Europeana. It recommends clear signposting in the creation of curated stories that are evocative and personal, with a specific focus, as well as facilitating multivocal experiences (Europeana Storytelling Task Force, 2021). Expertise is mentioned but balanced by the idea of stories having a more informal quality, suggesting the value of cultivating a different voice for Europeana, and minimizing the top-down technocratic tone often associated with the project (Valtysson, 2020). Effecting this change in tone also presents a challenge with regard to the collections, which largely comprise artworks, historical documents and manuscripts from GLAMs in EU member states, in other words authorized heritage (Smith, 2006). The organization of material on the website has changed over time, and the transnational bent is less overt than in earlier iterations of Europeana, indicating a move towards multivocality. The current landing page still contains a central search bar but, directly beneath this, users are given the option to search collections organized by Theme, or to click on the Stories feature which consists of Blogs Posts, Galleries, and Exhibitions. These are distinguished from one another by their narrative form; Blog Posts are shorter, telling a specific story, while Galleries and Exhibitions are narrated by images with the latter also including some interpretive text. Despite appearing under the heading of Stories, they do not directly utilize digital storytelling techniques and the task force report notes that more could be done to connect with current affairs and historical anniversaries (Europeana Storytelling Task Force, 2021). Europeana Collections, which serves as an alternative landing page for the site, is even less prescriptive and allows users to explore by Theme, Topic, Century, and Organization. The danger here is that, in its pursuit of curated content, Europeana has created an abundance of categories which dilute the focus required for effective narratives (DiBlasio and DiBlasio, 1983).

The tension between national heritage cultures and the creation of transnational narratives has not entirely receded in Europeana and the new Strategy touches on pan-European topics with the goal of transcending 'cultural and national borders (to) place collections in the European context' (Europeana, 2020: 17). The creation of narratives that highlight a 'European perspective' across cultural sectors has also appeared in policy documents relating to Europeana's role as a data space (EC, 2021b). Here, it is possible to see how the vision of a common European heritage links up with digital sovereignty and the EU's aim of utilizing cultural heritage data to attain a foothold in the global technology sector. As infrastructure, Europeana's role is not solely in the background, but also imagined as a distinctive marker and promoter of the European brand globally.

Conclusion

The EU's interests as a geopolitical entity aspiring towards a supranational, transnational identity are reflected in the changes Europeana has undergone during its lifespan. Europeana is an expression of digital geopolitics insofar as it reveals the political pursuit of harmonization and rationalization via technical means. This process has undergone various transformations; in its early years (2008–2011), Europeana was predominantly a digital library project, supported by experts in information systems, who concentrated on building its database and website. Later (2014–2020), because of its range of interests and partners, it was increasingly portrayed as a network of people and projects, using the platform metaphor to express its interaction between different, but interdependent, groups. Latterly (2020-present), Europeana has drawn attention to its role as infrastructure and a way of connecting and promoting European cultural heritage data.

In Europeana, it is the organization and standardization of information that supports the EC's assertion of a common European cultural heritage. The aggregator constitutes a technological solution to what is a political problem, namely, that of European federalism. This goal cannot be stated directly, but expresses itself through a continual reimagining of the European project, as Abélès discerns. He observes that EC officials 'prefer the delights of a future whose content they choose not to draw precisely. The care which is taken for erasing any sign of a political form yet to come [. . .] allows us to understand that New Europe, tomorrow's Europe, looks more like an ethereal dream than a utopia which could stir people into action' (2000: 34). The destination of virtual Europe is simultaneously assumed and denied in the EU project, in part because of its ambiguous mode of governance, in part because it hinges on a future that is not precisely defined. Such an uncertain future signals the unstable foundations upon which the idea of EU Europe rests. Because of this instability, the assertion of cultural 'Europeanness' has emerged as a preoccupation in projects like Europeana, which is underpinned by the normative values of the organization. The quest for digital sovereignty that has come to shape EU digital policy debates in recent years also has this normative dimension at its core, especially in terms of its attempts to regulate the contemporary information environment. These values are given life both as a technology and as a condition of European identity. The Europeana case study has provided an opening for exploring these issues, and shown how networked cultural resources and institutions operate within a larger geopolitical agenda of transnational integration and strategic autonomy.

5 Aggregating Global Heritage: Google Arts & Culture

Introduction

According to its Director, the Google Arts & Culture (GAC) programme started in the spirit of Google's 'Twenty Percent Time' policy with a simple question: 'How do you take all these different tools that Google has and alter them for the cultural sector?' (Caines, 2013) Employing high-resolution gigapixel photo-capturing technology and Google's Street View technology allowing users to explore museums virtually and zoom into famous paintings up-close, the first public showing of GAC took place in 2011. It featured only a thousand artefacts from seventeen of the world's most famous museums, such as New York's Metropolitan Museum of Art and Museum of Modern Art, London's National Gallery and Tate Britain, the Museo Reina Sofia in Madrid, and the Van Gogh Museum in Amsterdam, among others. However, only two years later GAC opened a dedicated Artists Lab in Paris where 'creative experts and technology come together, share ideas and build new ways to experience art and culture'. It has quickly transformed into 'a proper product within Google' – part of the not-for-profit foundation Google Cultural Institute. By that time, already partnering with 300 museums in 44 countries (Caines, 2013), the platform generated over 19 million unique visitors and 200 million page views annually (Wilson-Barnao, 2017). Rapidly multiplying agreements with museums around the world, in 2014 GAC added two architectural wonders to the portal – the Taj Mahal in India and Angkor Wat in Cambodia – expanding its digital offerings with two more pillars beyond art: architecture and archaeology, and promising to include the performance art in the future (Lee, 2014).

In 2015, while hosting almost five million artefacts from the collections of more than 850 art museums and historical archives, available in 18 languages, GAC presented to the world 360-degree videos as a part of an innovative assemblage of 60 performing arts groups. They included American Ballet Theater, the John F. Kennedy Center for the Performing Arts, the Metropolitan Opera, the Rome Opera and the Berlin Philharmonic (Sood, 2015). Two years later, the Director Amit Sood, boasted during his TED Talk that GAC used the power of machine learning and Artificial Intelligence (AI) to 'crack the problem of curating', introducing 'X Degrees' technology that allowed for the creation of multiple unexpected visual pathways and connections through around six million images of world cultural artefacts (Davis, 2017). Since 2015, a wide range of new applications have emerged on the platform, such as 'We Wear Culture', 'Once Upon and Try', 'Wonders of Indonesia' or 'Wonders of Mexico', which masterfully incorporate fashion, science, natural wonders, and all sorts of cultural tourist attractions to the GAC platform for users' enjoyment and exploration.

At the time of writing, in 2022, GAC holds agreements with 2000 cultural institutes in 80 countries across the world, covering all continents except Antarctica (GAC, 2022a). The COVID-19 global pandemic has only elevated the popularity of GAC as 'a go to' platform 'that makes art and places of cultural interest accessible to all, free of charge on the global scale' (Ross, 2022). Quadrupling its daily online searches, as was evidenced on Google Trends starting in March 2020 (Candeloro, 2021), GAC now generates around fourteen million unique visits every month (SW, 2022). Integrating GAC with such services as YouTube, Google+, GMail, Google Docs, and Google Maps, GAC made it possible for global audiences to connect with culture from different parts of the world through their gadgets without leaving their homes. Moreover, GAC offers a wide range of interactive experiences for learning, including virtual puzzles, colouring in art books, comparing cultural monuments across time, projecting 3D models into real-world environments, and even conducting virtual Google Expeditions (Cowin, 2020).

On the institutional side, GAC provides new affordances to cultural institutions to digitize, share and display their collections, resources, and performances in the context of increasing funding cuts and a more competitive economic environment. However, what is the real cost of 'playing' with digital heritage on GAC? What is the trade-off for cultural institutions and their audiences to enjoy 'the world's art and culture online' that has become 'accessible to anyone, anywhere' (GAC, 2022b). This section argues that GAC, while aiming for universal accessibility of cultural information and using the rhetoric of cultural democratization, inclusivity, and participation, is building a global monopoly and pushing forward the forces of neocolonial cultural imperialism in the context of neoliberal platform capitalism.

Building a Monopoly: Digital Heritage Imperialism

By promoting universal access to knowledge, culture, and heritage across languages and communities, Google is, in fact, building a powerful monopoly in the global media space (de Largy Healy and Glowczewski, 2014). Being a powerful global corporation, Google, as a predominantly profit-making actor, aims to maximize returns on its investments and extend its penetration to wider information markets (Elad, 2010). This strategy is evidenced in its extensive material infrastructure, which is a precondition of Google's astronomical geographical expansion and capital accumulation. Today, Google has more than eighty-eight offices in over forty-two countries around the globe (Google, 2022a). Its search engine runs in 348 languages (WEF, 2015), covering up to 90 per cent of search markets globally (Statista, 2022). To keep their 'products running 24 hours a day, 7 days a week', across continents, in the past decade it tripled the number of its data centres, reaching 32 centres (Google, 2022b) and built a network of 173 Cloud locations available across 35 regions, 106 zones, and more than 200 countries around the world (Google, 2022c). If these estimates, collected from the Google website, are even partially correct, the possibility of a serious competitor to Google in the global media market is quite difficult to imagine. For example, in 2018 alone, Google invested more than 100 million dollars in developing the technology and the licensing agreements for its YouTube channel, which introduced considerable financial and legal barriers for all potential competitors to the video hosting market (Gray, 2020).

Google's infrastructural superiority is only a result of its business model's success, based on the most efficient search engine in the world. Its secret, though, is not necessarily a magic algorithm that delivers to users' the best search results; rather, it is based on the company's exclusive access to large repositories of information. In 2011, Google's Chief Scientist Peter Norvig shared: 'We don't have better algorithms than anyone else; we just have more data' (Gray, 2020: 136). Google Search, Google Images, and Google Books, for instance, operate on exclusive access to content from the public domain and third-party ownership. This data feeds Google algorithms to find patterns in user behaviour, supplying valuable insights for advertisers who contribute to most of Google's profits.

According to historian George Dyson, when speaking to a Google engineer about the Google Books project, he revealed: 'We are not scanning all those books to be read by people. We are scanning them to be read by AI' (2012: 87). Google is appropriating cultural materials on a global scale to maintain its exclusive access to a vast dataset of computer readable metadata, used to train algorithms and to develop new products and services to maximize its income (Cheney-Lippold, 2011; Hillis et al., 2012; Gillespie, 2014). As Shawn M. Powers and Michael Jablonski stress, Google's success and its astronomical market dominance is based on its ability 'to identify and extract nondigital, real-space data into a form that is usable and helpful [. . .] through the conversion of existing information (books, museum archives, maps, houses, businesses, and so on) into digital, searchable formats' (2015: 84).

Viewed in this light, even though GAC is promoted as a philanthropic cultural initiative to open up museums and their collections to the world, it is another platform for Google to extract, refine, interpret and consolidate its monopolistic access to cultural data globally. Suhair Khan, the Lead on the Google Arts & Culture projects and collaborations in one of the interviews, shared: 'Art and Culture is important to Google because it is a critical part of the world's shared history and social fabric'. She stressed that 'the aims of Google Arts & Culture are in line with Google's broader mission to organize and make accessible the world's information', which, indeed, would remain incomplete without global cultural heritage (Gajardo and Lau, 2017). Furthermore, as Amit Sood, GAC Director, shared, the omnivorous ambition and global quest for more organized and useful information drove the development of the GAC platform, that started with the digitization of museums' artworks and 'become a much larger project':

> We've gone beyond art into performing arts, natural history, world monuments and historic sites. We're incorporating intangible cultural heritage; things that you can't touch and see in a museum. It's a much more challenging but rewarding experience. It's about culture as a broader narrative. (Sharma, 2017)

While Google's mission stresses its priority to provide users with universal access to the information they need, its business model directly depends on the successful connections established among advertisers with valuable consumers, based on analysis of large quantities of accurate, longitudinal user data (Powers and Jablonski, 2015). Collecting and channelling consumers' data on their cultural activities and interests in different parts of the world reveals the commercial logic implied even in the non-profit initiative of the GAC platform. As explained by Wilson-Barnao, digital copies of artefacts provide an exceptionally rich source for generating users' personal behaviour data as 'people respond to the aesthetic and historical content by playing with it and circulating it through their social networks online or simply by viewing it' (2017: 559). Online engagements with cultural objects on GAC monetize sentiments, emotions, and experiences evoked in global viewers by cultural material and furnish algorithms with users' behavioural data concerning their tastes and preferences to analyse and understand their personal profiles and predict their future behaviour.

In this regard, the push forward for global coverage of digital heritage from different corners of the world is strategic. A part of the global museum community, the author has encountered GAC regional coordinators and digitization specialists participating at major international museum and heritage conferences around the world at least since 2012. Their presentations expose museum professionals to digitization tools that Google makes available to its partners for free, including Tabletop Scanner, Art Camera with ultra-high-resolution image capturing and Museum View, which can create virtual tours around museum premises. They promote the value for cultural institutions of joining the GAC platform by adding their cultural resources to the global repository of digital heritage. These conference presentations are only one part of the global outreach strategy to conquer new markets with regional offices spreading to Latin America, Africa, and Asia Pacific.

An interview with a regional coordinator in Southeast Asia revealed that adding new museums to the platform is not sporadic and not necessarily based on the personal connections of coordinators, who usually come from the target regions. 'It's kind of a bit more complex than that,' the Asia GAC Manager explained. 'While we do receive inquiries, we also have road maps where we want to develop more. So, in such cases, then we would initiate target outreaches activities,' that could start from a mere phone call, then progressing to museum visits with presentations and demos and even training sessions delivered to museum staff (RCA, 2022). Signing a contract with a museum to join GAC sometimes takes up to two years or even longer, but it is a part of the regional coordinators' jobs to 'continue the conversations to build relationships' with heritage partners to penetrate target areas. GAC Lead Khan also flagged that it is Google's strategy to ensure they are working with their regional partners around the world 'at their pace, to their needs and ensuring we are helping make their visions a reality through technology' (Gajardo and Lau, 2017).

Back in 2011 at the very start of the project, GAC Director Sood explained that once museums are ready, Google takes full responsibility 'to provide all resources totally for free' to take care of the different operations, including the recording of the selected museum halls with the street view trolley, taking the high resolution and the gigapixel photographs, or uploading the metadata (Zheleva, 2011). The appeal of taking advantage of free digitization technologies and resources worked excellently in the past decade to bring thousands of museums on board, especially considering cultural heritage digitization often progresses slowly as quite a challenging, resource-demanding, and time-consuming process. Even in Europe by 2017, 82 per cent of small museums had digitized less than half of their collections with 67 per cent of museums having less than 25 per cent of their digital preservation completed (Amato et al., 2017). In 2018, the percentage of museum digital objects available online across Russia as related to analogue collections constituted only 1.5 per cent of all total museum collections. In Saint Petersburg alone museums had only

1 per cent of digital images available online as related to the total number of all museum objects in their collections (Kizhner et al., 2018).

Interviews with museum professionals participating in the GAC programme, conducted by Udell (2019), revealed that even the US museums are primarily interested in using the platform to digitize their content and improve access to their collections. In fact, the features which museums reported as most useful just before the pandemic were the same as GAC originally offered in 2011: Museum View and the gigapixel Art Camera's zoom feature. The author's numerous interviews with museum professionals around the world, from the first museum from Canada who joined GAC, Musée McCord, to partnering museums in Indonesia, Malaysia, and Singapore, who joined more recently, have resulted in similar observations. The primary logic behind heritage institutions' involvement with GAC concerns addressing the digitization agenda to increase collections' accessibility, as well as to develop a more robust institutional brand to attract new audiences. However, this logic, stressing the value of outsourcing and delegating collections access to a corporate giant, highlights the influence and concentration of corporate control over human heritage that belongs to the public.

While the digitization of heritage collections through GAC activities makes them more accessible to local and international audiences, meeting the long-standing goals of many museums, GAC is designed primarily to facilitate consumption, and not a cultural co-creation as could erroneously be assumed. On the one hand, by directly increasing public access to information, including cultural heritage, and by providing participatory online tools for audiences to experiment and play with artefacts and exhibitions, Google democratizes culture and increases opportunities for participation in meaning-making. On the other hand, it primarily secures its own exclusive access to vast cultural assets and information that gives the corporation an unassailable advantage in global media markets. With its ambition 'to organize the world's information and make it universally accessible' Google is a critical dominant information provider and a global monopoly. In many cases it serves as an information gatekeeper that can curate 'search results according to numerous factors and principles' (Gray, 2020: 145), thus shaping and controlling the social realities of global audiences (Jiang, 2013).

Academic scholarship has discussed how Google manipulates its search results, exercising discretionary power and acting in response to its own and collaborators' interests (Gray, 2020). Even more dangerous, though, is the negative aspect of gatekeeping, such as a mainstreaming effect that is the result of search algorithms popularizing certain content, while marginalizing others (Richey and Taylor 2017: 29). GAC, for instance, was criticized in academia and accused of 'digital cultural colonialism' for its lack of balance, with Western countries and institutions being prioritized on the platform and with a high proportion of the holdings featuring content that resides primarily in the United States (Kizhner et al., 2021). Wani (2019) also indicated that the top ten artists and collections on GAC belong to the United States and Europe as dominant regions which are the most comprehensively presented in all sections of the collections. GAC's editorial feature, ranking a handful of European and US museums as the 'top museums' and pushing them up on the list of participating institutions, demonstrates an abuse of curatorial power, as Valtysson observes (Valtysson, 2020). 'Google Arts & Culture platform is not an open one like Youtube,' a representative of one of Singapore's museums shared, 'we have little control and do contribute, but Google treats it like their own curated showcase. We don't get to augment it as freely. As such you'll see that it actually isn't inclusive, as many museums, especially smaller or Southeast Asian ones might not be represented' (NGSR, 2023).

When challenged with the observation of such an imbalance, GAC Director Sood, in one of his interviews explained,

> 'We talk about the culture sector with a very American and European bias, and that's because a lot of the leading museums and galleries in the world are based in Paris, New York and so on. But when you start travelling to the other cultural hubs – Korea, Japan, Australia, Brazil, Mexico – everyone is at a different understanding of what the web can do for them. We're just not there as yet' (Caines, 2013).

While it could be argued that Google strives to add cultural content from different countries around the world and it is only a matter of time before it penetrates regions in Latin America, Africa, and Asia, GAC remains a dominant producer of non-scholarly 'infrastructures of knowledge-making', reproducing already existing biases in cultural representations (Mansfield, 2014; Bode, 2020). These cultural representations appear as particularly threatening, especially considering that in a recent book, *Under Discussion: The Encyclopedic Museum*, featuring interviews with world's top museum directors, Sood compared GAC with 'a true "encyclopaedia" of art' that could document and cross-index the contents of virtually every museum and art collection on the planet. 'While it will never be complete,' Sood asserted, 'it is always going to be my goal to try to make it as comprehensive as possible, and we will never stop' (Grau, 2021: 155).

Sood also stressed GAC's democratic potential to 'flatten' notional hierarchies, arguing that on the platform 'all museums and all objects are equal [...] where you can go to the British Museum, then just suddenly find your way into a museum that maybe you had never heard of' (Grau, 2021: 153). However, as Kizhner et al. point out, 'Data on less visible cultures continue to be distorted and invisible, and cultural layers that are given less prominence are withdrawn' (2021: 630). According to Van Dijck et al., aggregated digital content is a powerful tool 'producing the social structures we live in' (2018: 3). The digital infrastructure offered by the platform and algorithms which produce more information of similar content (Zuboff, 2019) represent the epistemologies of dominant countries. They shape informational realities of the world, while amplifying existing biases and strengthening cultural prejudices (Kizhner et al., 2021). As a result, a highly unbalanced data representation leads to the streaming of cultural capital across ethnic, economic, and social groups, and can eventually incite cross-cultural mistrust and even conflicts (Bertrand and Kamenica, 2018). In its media representations, Google is argued to be 'unable to guarantee its objectivity [. . .] without discrimination, regardless of the place depicted, and the determination of political labels', thereby transcending the realm of micro-geopolitics and obtaining 'a geopolitical subjectivity per se' (Turčalo and Kulović, 2018: 18). The next section reveals the geopolitical ambitions and strategies of Google as a corporate actor in the international arena.

Google Geopolitics: A Transnational Media Corporation on the World Stage

Google's cultural activities on the world stage have been subject to the criticism of neo-colonialism, and are not geopolitically neutral. They are, in fact, closely aligned with US foreign policy strategies and agendas (CFA, 2019). It is important to note that Google is confined by American legal regulations, due to the company's origin and its compulsory compliance with US markets, laws, and practices. Throughout the company's history, Google has been increasingly active in US international relations, with the State Department acting 'to outsource part of its public diplomacy mission to the company' (Gustin, 2013). For example, Google carried out numerous projects in close cooperation with Washington, helping to advance American Internet and advocacy projects that 'were too sensitive for overt efforts by the U.S. government . . . There are things the private sector can do that the U.S. government can't do', Jared Cohen explained. Cohen is a former Chief Architect of the State Department's Internet-Freedom Doctrine, who in 2010 joined Google as the Director of Google Ideas (Larson, 2010). 'While it seems clear that Googlers do genuinely support freedom of expression as a fundamental human right, there is little evidence that this is the reason the company pursues greater global connectivity' (Powers & Jablonski, 2015: 97).

While pursuing its global market expansion as its business strategy, Google, unsurprisingly, finds itself 'on the front lines of the cyber war, advocating for increased openness and connectivity around the world, including in North Korea, Afghanistan, Pakistan, and Burma' (Powers and Jablonski, 2015: 74). In fact, its expansion into different parts of the developing world and advocacy against censorship in authoritarian countries closely align with the State Department's 'freedom-to-connect agenda' (CFA, 2019). For example, in the famous case of 'withdrawal' from China, despite Google's public claim of moral superiority and an ongoing criticism of totalitarian censorship, it has 'never given up on its efforts to gain market share in the world's largest Internet market' (Yeo, 2016: 599). Both Google and the US Government's provocation of China on censorship and media freedom is only a way to pressure China to further open the Internet market to US capital (Yeo, 2016). This is exactly why in 2012 Daniel Alegre, Google's Asia-Pacific Operations President, revealed: 'We never left China [. . .] It's a very vibrant Internet market. We have some of the best employees at Google and we continue to grow not only our revenue but also our headcount in the country' (Li and Womack, 2012).

Remaining active in China is part of the larger global strategy of building 'infrastructure of extraterritorial information networks', which is critical for the expansion of capitalist economies (Hunt, 2010). Considering that processes are complex and conflicted, as various stakeholders' interests are directly involved, Google tries offering something different in order to compete with local giants among Internet providers, like Baidu, that holds almost 60 per cent of China's search engine market (SC, 2022). In the past decade, GAC has signed agreements with Chinese heritage institutions in Beijing, Shanghai, Hubei, Sichuan, and Yunnan and features collections from of forty-two partners, ranging from traditional museums like the National Silk Museum to those most recently developed, such as UCCA of Beijing's famous 798 Art District (Jin, 2022). It even includes artworks from the Palace Museum in Beijing, one of the most significant icons of national culture and one of China's foremost protected cultural heritage sites (Li et al., 2014). Moreover, in 2021, GAC offered a 360-degree virtual tour of the Great Wall of China, showcasing the Simatai section of the Great Wall. Stanley Chen, President of Google Greater China, shared that progress in China in the past several years has been impressive: 'We are very proud to be able to help share the broad and profound cultural assets of China with more users around the world through technology and innovation' (Jin, 2022).

Discussing further these powers of Google to manage international relations, Hunt (2010) defines Google as a key non-state actor in international affairs, a company that pursues corporate interests on the world stage, either in tandem with the US Government or not. Some scholars go further, arguing that Google is not simply a global economic actor, but is a rival power to existing nation-states (Medeiros, 2021). Interestingly, in 2017, Denmark announced a new Government position for a Digital Ambassador to liaise with some of the world's top tech companies, including Google, Apple, and Microsoft (Gramer, 2017). In his interview, Foreign Minister Anders Samuelsen explained: 'These companies have become a type of new nations and we need to confront that [. . .] We will of course maintain our old way of thinking in which we foster our relationships with other countries. But we simply need to have closer ties to some of the companies that affect us' (Gramer, 2017).

Indeed, working directly with governments and intergovernmental organizations, like UNESCO, Google reveals its ambitious geopolitical focus to operate at the international level as a premier digital platform for aggregating cultural heritage. In 2009, for example, Google signed an alliance agreement with UNESCO to create a global online platform for virtual visits to World Heritage Sites via Google Earth and Google Maps interfaces. As UNESCO's Director-General Irina Bokova explained, this collaboration aims to 'increase awareness and to encourage participation in the preservation of these treasures' (UNESCO, 2009). Since then, Google has been working with the UNESCO World Heritage Centre to make World Heritage accessible to everyone virtually, bringing cultural and natural treasures directly into everyone's home. In 2020 World Heritage sites have been added to GAC, and two years later they have been enhanced with stories through the launch of the International Register of selected items which 'shaped humanity's shared past' (UNESCO, 2022).The case of collaboration with UNESCO is illustrative of Google's imperialistic position, which is not only about its technological superiority but also about massive digital aggregation and appropriation of the humanity's cultural heritage.

Google's constant global expansion is in line with the UNESCO World Heritage Sites (WHS) programme's agenda which is also a global phenomenon, although it is charged with 'complex multinational and bureaucratic procedures that accompany such designations' in different countries around the world (Glovine, 2008: 71). Since 1972, when the Convention Concerning the Protection of the World Cultural and Natural Heritage was signed, WHS has grown into a complex political machinery of heritage global governance which operates through conflicting and contradicting mechanisms. On the one hand, it aspires for 'universal' protection, celebration, and promotion of heritage sites, matching perfectly Google's mission 'to organize the world's information and make it universally accessible and useful'. On the other hand, this endeavour to apply a 'universal value' to heritage sites and 'rework territorial conceptions in the minds of its global populous through the promotion of a new and universally understood intellectual and cultural conceptualization of the world' is at odds with the aspirations of nation-states involved in the programme to help with heritage protection on the ground (Glovine, 2008: 73). By contrast, in its attempt to create a 'homogenizing' sense of place, the WHS programme reconceptualizes the spatial, temporal, and living connections of heritage sites to their local history and contexts.

Criticized for its Eurocentrism (Labadi, 2005; Bui and Lee, 2015) and its 'legacy of colonialism and impending neo-imperialistic advances' (Kersel and Luke, 2015), this international legal regime for the protection of cultural heritage could be seen as contributing to 'cultural degradation' (Shepherd, 2006) and even 'cultural destruction' (Macmillan, 2017). It results from heritage exoticization and commodification through the growth of national tourism (Ashworth, 1994), as well as from heritage politicization, stemming from nation-states' ideological imperatives aiming either for nation-building, decolonization or simply for economic recovery and development (Bui and Lee, 2015). UNESCO's idealized worldview of culture, politics, and world heritage, as reflected in WHS objectives, creates dissonance with instrumental approaches of involved stakeholders, including nation-states seeking designations and global popularization of their heritage resources, and Google, pursuing its imperialistic programme for world information extraction and aggregation. For them, culture and heritage become just a resource for new forms of capital accumulation in the conditions of global neoliberalism, driven by market demands and information technologies (Coombe and Weiss, 2015). Embedded in GAC's geopolitical rationale and the economic logic of cultural platformization (Jin, 2017), such a massive digital heritage aggregation in collaboration with UNESCO works not only for Google's capital accumulation but also for the global expansion of its power.

Implications of Heritage Platformization

The platformization of the world's cultural heritage perpetuates processes of digital heritage commodification. It is evident in the GAC's logic, primarily driven by Sood's vision to reach larger global audiences to increase the consumption of digital heritage among users 'who would be unlikely to visit the homes (or even the home pages) of the Paris Opera, the Royal Shakespeare Company or Carnegie Hall' (Cooper, 2015). During his TED talk he stressed that there are many ways people find their pathways to arts and culture, and the GAC's mission is to create more opportunities for a regular user to find their own route to cultural heritage by making it more attractive (TED, 2017). 'For some people, a very long curatorial narrative on impressionist art will not work. But if I say: hey, you want to see what bling used to be like in 1800? I think there's a lot of opportunity for disruption, for changing people's minds,' Sood remarked (Davis, 2017).

In GAC, the process of heritage consumption is underpinned by two strategies; first, the expansion of cultural experiences from high arts to pop culture; and second, the intensification of experiences through the use of AI and new media technologies for gamification. With regard to the former, Sood (2022) has emphasized: 'Yes, there is the Mona Lisa, but there is also Nigerian pepper soup, Australian sporting culture, Indonesian batik or graffiti in the streets of Brazil and beyond. This expanded our sense of culture and enriched our understanding of humankind.' Expanding GAC to embrace all forms and manifestations of cultures that a global traveller might encounter in different parts of the world, GAC perfectly accommodates contemporary tourists' demands and trends of 'place collection' and 'place consumption' (Urry, 1995). GAC created new affordances for digital consumption, collection, and experience of cultural sites and natural environments, expanding its offerings to include pop culture. For instance, it comes as no surprise that most recently Google tapped into the power of Korean Wave to attract a multimillion global K-Pop audience by establishing a collaboration with the popular music group BTS through the 'BTS x Street Galleries' project. It takes fans on a virtual Street View tour of the cities and buildings holding special BTS memories and featuring 'artworks curated by the band, based on values that are close to their heart' (Peter-Agbia, 2022).

Employing pop culture as a resource to drive visitation, GAC not only expands its audiences at the expense of dumbing down values of human heritage, more importantly, the platform subjects it further to 'disneyfication processes'. This is defined as removing negative or inconvenient narratives and replacing them with idealized tourist-friendly representations, which threaten to obscure and obliterate human understanding of what heritage is (Malpas, 2007). Similarly to analogue transformations of heritage into 'present-era leisure sites and potentially lucrative tourist attractions', GAC's representation of heritage with a global consumer's demands and interests in mind tends towards historical simplification, creating entertaining online 'theme-parks' 'of a "scientifically" imagined past' (McCrary, 2011: 360).

The World Wonders programme, under the patronage of UNESCO, offers an excellent example. It draws on Street View technology to take visitors 'on a virtual trip to each iconic site' as well as including 3D models and YouTube videos of historical places to allow online users to explore traditions, tangible and intangible heritage resources, and virtually experience natural wonders (Blaschke, 2012). Its landing page is an infinite scrolling list of offerings welcoming online visitors to 'enjoy la dolce vita in Italy', 'explore towns in South America', 'walk around places of worship' from Peru to Indonesia, go inside mystical temples in different parts of the world, or 'jump into the wild of landscapes that take your breath away' (GAC, 2023). With its glossy marketing design, saturated images, seductive language and presentation, the online page is reminiscent of a pile of advertising brochures in a tourist agency. Indeed, utilizing the digital placemaking and digital tourism potential of GAC is a growing trend among various tourism departments in different countries, to generate cultural awareness of small urban locales, driven by economic goals to 'help employment, sustainable economic growth, poverty reduction, environmental protection and the preservation of authenticity in cultural heritage' (Pascoal et al., 2019: 55).

For instance, in 2021 Google launched Wonders of Vietnam, a country which after the pandemic has been pursuing a strategy of tourism recovery. In a media interview, Sood revealed that this project was welcomed and even 'encouraged by the local team and wonderful partners who were so passionate about showing the world the wonders of Vietnam' (TTN, 2021). 'It is an important part of Google's overall support of the local tourism industry', the GAC Director asserted, especially in conditions when it 'has been badly affected by pandemic-related travel restrictions' (TTN, 2021). Heritage tourism, particularly in Asian countries, has exploded in recent years (Meskell and Brumann, 2015). Since 1986, the tourist industry has become one of Vietnam's key economic sectors, contributing by 2017 up to 8 per cent to the national GDP (WB, 2019) and welcoming up to eighteen million international visitors in 2019 alone (MT, 2022). UNESCO World Heritage Sites designations played a major part in the process of transforming Vietnam into the most rapidly developing tourist economy in Asia (Quang et al., 2022).

This development came with negative implications for local heritage and communities, marginalizing locals and ethnic minority groups and replacing 'often problematic and conflicting narratives' of heritage sites with 'a universalizing meta-narrative', crafted for global consumption (Glovine, 2008). Heritage dissonance, inherent in the process of resource selection, reinterpretation, and targeting for international tourism, in many cases destroyed local spiritual practices, authentic community experiences and transformed genuine festival events (Bui and Lee, 2015; Quang et al., 2022). These processes of 'cultural degradation' are replicated on GAC through the Wonders of Vietnam project that claims in Sood's words to 'capture the spirit of Vietnam' by making the experience of virtual travelling 'fun and interactive' (TTN, 2021). Indeed, the colour filter app, which allows users to explore Vietnam by colour, aerial 360-degree images of heritage sites from a bird's-eye view, sightseeing with a Vietnamese soundtrack, and even a playful quiz (GAC, 2022d) only reinforce the Disneyfication effects of Vietnam heritage presentation on the platform.

This Disneyfication process also works via heritage gamification that GAC particularly celebrates through its famous Artist Lab in Paris where 'techies become the new artists' (Sood, 2022). Featuring up to a hundred 'experiments at the crossroads of art and technology, created by Artists and Creative Coders', GAC provides various ways to 'play' with culture from exploring a interactive 3D landscapes created by AI, to organizing thousands of artworks by visual similarity, to creating music through a virtual paint brush translating images into musical notes performed by an instrument of choice, to navigating an atlas of emotions to understand how artworks are connected with feelings (GAC, 2022c). The experiments place cultural collections outside of the institutional structures of museums and are presented in a mobile device-friendly format that allows individuals to see them 'through new lenses'. While, to certain degree, they do democratize culture, offering new avenues for global audiences to discover playful ways to enjoy art, critic and scholar Ben Davies (2016), in reviewing tech experiments on the GAC platform, shared: 'Instead of proposing hidden depths, it seems to reduce all of art history to surface. The technical sophistication of these Experiments is in direct proportion to the primitiveness of the attempt to make meaning with them' (Davies, 2016).

Leaving alone the artistic value of experiments that could be argued to be questionable, the gamification of human heritage in GAC intensifies cultural commodification and folds into Google's ambition to engage more audiences or consumers on the global scale. In this process, both human heritage and online audiences become mere commodities for Google. Museum artefacts on GAC come to users' digital attention as manifestations that exist to be applied to a user's own interests and preferences. 'A piece of code can be used to augment the user's own identity, and therefore the collection begins to circulate through social media in new ways in the form of augmented faces rather than the original object' (Wilson-Barnao, 2021: 69).

Cultural heritage turns into promotional material, a mere background design that is adjusted to users' online expressions and practices, which is then shared widely through social media. Wani et al. (2019) also argue that GAC, with its experiments shuffling around millions of images derived from museums around the world, appears to be 'a gigantic voting, re-contextualization and marketing machine' that handles cultural heritage content without caring about 'academic degrees, institutional status or proper context' (115). At the same time, GAC users become online heritage consumers and direct subjects to 'surveillance capitalism', where 'populations are targets of data extraction' (Zuboff, 2019: 86). GAC's new offerings and services become valuable tools to engage online users, either genuine art lovers or just casual web surfers looking for leisure and entertainment. Expanding further on the global scale in terms of both cultural content appropriation and conquering new online consumer markets, GAC is a powerful vehicle for Google on its journey to a global monopoly of planetary cyberspace.

Conclusion

The phenomenon of GAC that brings together human heritage across countries, communities, and cultural institutions in one space is the result of unfolding platform imperialism existing in the conditions of neoliberal capitalism. It emerges at the crossroads of two overlapping processes. The first concerns heritage institutions' economic survivalism based on the growing necessity to find sustainable means and resources to support their agenda of collections' access and public sharing. The second is the ambition and strategy of global media corporations, like Google, to control and penetrate larger international markets to maximize their profits. Unlike other cases discussed in previous sections, GAC is the manifestation of a corporate actor's attempt to aggregate human cultural heritage in pursuit of its geopolitical goals and ambitions. These goals aim at no less than building a powerful monopoly of cultural digital infrastructure that can generate economic value by animating cultural content through digitization and gamification. At the same time, GAC creates reliable pathways for users to expose their personal preferences and interest for more careful data analysis and prediction.

More importantly, the platform is deeply involved in geopolitics serving as a corporate non-state actor in international relations. Closely collaborating with the US Government, especially when it makes economic sense, and pursuing its own interests on the global stage, Google employs its cultural heritage aggregator GAC to navigate the complexities of closed political regimes and censorship systems to penetrate larger international markets and conquer new audiences. With its top-tier intellectual talent, its massive financial resources, and its world-class analytic capabilities, Google operates on the world stage as 'a nation-state', or even as 'a virtual nation' (Hunt, 2010: 108). With its multicultural cosmopolitan corporate culture and strategy, cherry-picking from some of the world's best and brightest experts in data mining, information retrieval, design and programming, robotics and machine learning, it operates across cultural, social, linguistic borders and can boast to adhere to 'the gold standard in international accessibility' (Conti, 2009: 4).

Continuing the metaphor of a 'a virtual nation-state', one could conceptualize GAC as a department or bureau of international cultural affairs. In fact, it works directly with governments, cultural institutions, and heritage communities around the world, pursuing global causes of heritage preservation, sharing cultural resources with publics across borders and celebrating a myriad of cultures from pop and mainstream, like K-Pop, to marginalized ones like the Aboriginal people of Palawa Country in Australia. Moreover, it is engaged in long-term relationships with all stakeholders, ensuring that content appropriation goes beyond the digitization of a few artworks from museums, and steadily expands to different forms and manifestations of human cultures, intersecting with other domains of human life like science or tourism. Similarly to other digital heritage aggregators, devised and developed by governmental and intergovernmental actors, GAC promotes its own politics and ideology. This politics, though, does not aim to legitimize, promote, or celebrate a specific national or regional culture and identity. Instead, it promotes forces of neoliberal capitalism, operating in the twenty-first century through platform imperialism and subjecting human heritage, culture, and experiences to processes of digitized commodification.

6 Conclusion

Following Marshall McLuhan's famous phrase 'the medium is the message', it could be argued that technologies of digital heritage aggregation persistently influence how people conceive and experience their historical past and how they understand their future. This Element has demonstrated that the digitization of human heritage creates new modes of public memory production and consumption, as well as offering new avenues for constructing and sustaining 'imagined communities' and shaping the geographies of contemporary politics. The sections mapped and analysed four cases of digital heritage aggregators, which illustrate key principles of contemporary digital geopolitics, especially in relation to human heritage and culture. Even though these cases vary in their geographical focus and scope, not to mention their organizational structure, content, and heritage preservation architectures, all of them are evidence that online heritage spaces are highly politically engaged sites of ideological manipulations, representative of their stakeholders' geopolitical agendas and ambitions. While questions of digital heritage policy and politics have been explored insightfully in the academic scholarship (Bonde Thylstrup, 2018; Valtysson, 2020), this Element offers a distinctive geopolitical perspective.

First, the volume identified and analysed several principles of geopolitical representation with regard to the construction of spatial realities through digital heritage, including *building digital sovereignty* on national and supranational levels, *virtual enlargement*, and *digital imperialism*. Second, the case studies encompassed a wide geopolitical scope, from small nation-states, such as Singapore, to global digital heritage, as in the case of Google. This range highlights the complexity of contemporary geopolitics in terms of involved actors from nation-states, to intergovernmental organizations, to transnational corporations. Here, it was shown that they operate according to different economic and political imperatives, pursuing distinct agendas, from *digital heritage politicization* to *digital heritage monetization*. However, in all cases the accumulation of heritage, under the patronage of either governments or a private corporation, raised important questions of digital heritage aggregators' sustainability as platforms of public memory preservation for future generations. This concluding section aims to contemplate and elaborate on these issues to suggest further avenues for a more sustainable and equitable future for digital heritage, recognizing that it will always remain vulnerable in relation to state support and private funding.

Digital Technologies of Spatial Production

'The technological construction of reality is as valid a notion as is the social construction of reality' (Timmers, 2022). The four case studies illustrate that digital heritage aggregators provide important platforms for the technological production of geopolitical realities, from securing the legitimacy of contested geographical territories to global, imperialistic domination and monopolization. The first three cases engaged with the phenomenon of digital legitimacy to varying degrees. For example, the Singapore Memory Project (SMP) serves the Singapore Government as a reliable platform for establishing the country's cultural legitimacy to leverage its identity and negotiate its interests in the global context. 'Singapore's maturity as a city-state in the global context has also given rise to a critical need and urgency in ensuring that the Singapore story is collected and discovered' (Pin, 2014: 63). A young and still emerging nation, Singapore in the past decade was driven to collect, preserve, and promote national cultural heritage that can serve as evidence of its very existence in the international arena.

Being very limited, both in its actual physical territory and in cultural heritage assets that could represent the highly multicultural composition of the constructed Singaporean nation, the SMP employs *virtual enlargement* as a geopolitical technology of space production. A strategic attempt to augment its areas of regional domination and importance in a wider global community, this national digital heritage project serves two main functions. First, the digital heritage aggregator offers a platform to create propagandistic online representations of Singapore as a 'gateway to Asia', disproportionately large in relation to its actual physical size. Second, while engendering a compensatory symbolic power, crowdsourced public contributions accumulated through the SMP aim to legitimize and naturalize Singaporean identity to make it an object of national pride and celebration. The technological infrastructure of the project heavily relies on public heritage aggregation and individual participation of both residents and international visitors and is representative of the strategy of virtual enlargement. This manifests in its quantifiable, ambitious, and illusory goal to collect '5 million memories', which was never achieved; in comparison, Google currently hosts six million images of artefacts from around the world. It is evident in the SMP's highly international outlook as well. Aiming to engage international audiences, the project either invited visitors to share their own memories of experiencing Singapore or simply targeted them by selling an appealing travel destination to experience the cultural wealth and breadth of Asia in one go.

Both inward and outward trajectories of geopolitical representation are also at play in the construction of a national heritage aggregator such as Australia's Trove. Developing from a tool for discovering heritage, Trove has grown in the past decade to the status of national heritage infrastructure. Its national ambition, in this case to become 'Australia's sovereign cultural resource' (NLA, 2021: 14), works through the geopolitical space production strategy of establishing *digital sovereignty*, operating via two complementary dynamics. On the one hand, aiming to leverage its leadership position in the contested Asia-Pacific region, Trove is prone to complex geopolitical shifts in Australia's navigation of relationships with surrounding countries. Excluding or including, for instance, Chinese sources and collections in the national heritage infrastructure fluctuates and mirrors the country's foreign policy agenda, whereby the economic and military rise of China is celebrated as opportunity, or by contrast positioned as a threat to national security.

On the other hand, the Australian Government, in a similar way to Singapore, strives to create a cohesive image of the nation, grappling with and very much affected by historical colonial legacies. The multicultural composition of the nation builds on numerous waves of immigration, bringing together difficult and contested histories, not so easily presented within a single digital heritage space. Seeking its legitimacy in constituting a democratic society, Australia is also challenged by its colonial past and the issue of First Nations inclusion into the social fabric of the nation. Reflecting these complexities, Trove exemplifies an attempt to address national debates on Indigenous heritage, while struggling with a digital infrastructure that can thoroughly deliver equitable cultural governance and shared authority with the First Nation communities who have their own claims to sovereignty.

The strategy of establishing a *digital sovereignty* escalates to the transnational level in the case of Europeana, a digital heritage aggregator that aims to legitimize the European Union (EU) as a single geopolitical entity aspiring towards a unified supranational identity. In pursuit of political harmonization and rationalization, Europeana, which transformed from the proposal for a digital library into a digital regional infrastructure, is based on the EU's ambition to organize and standardize information that supports the assertion of a common European cultural heritage. The technical architecture of the aggregator brings millions of digital artefacts from heritage institutions across Europe together in one space, striving to realize the 'unity in diversity' aspiration of the EU project. Caught within the complexity of its own diversity, manifesting in cultural, linguistic, socio-economic, historico-political, and technological disintegrations and internal conflicts within the region and neighbouring countries, Europeana exemplifies a heritage quest for digital sovereignty.

This drive chimes with how EU digital policy debates have evolved over the past decade. There is now a regional agenda to establish regulations in the contemporary information environment, especially in the global context of threats of domination from more powerful actors. 'Once an economic giant (but a political dwarf), Europe's ambitions for the "digital decade" are caught in between a duopoly with the USA and China dominating the global digital economy' (Werthner, 2022: 243). Launched as a direct response to the Google Books project with the aim of maintaining control over European cultural heritage, Europeana now strives to attain digital sovereignty through the creation of protected data spaces (EC, 2021a). It attempts to promote its humanistic values in an evolving global digital ecosystem, where Google, Amazon, Facebook, Apple, and Microsoft, as well as the Chinese Baidu, Alibaba, and Tencent are powerful new actors, in many cases with revenues much larger than EU countries' GDPs (Metakides, 2022). To survive in this competitive digital reality, the EU needs to coordinate 'three basic instruments, investment, regulation, and completion of the digital internal market', which are subject to the financial capabilities of Europe, and are rapidly declining, due to economic instability (Metakides, 2022: 219).

At a time when national governments' and intergovernmental organizations' support for digital heritage aggregation is in decline, corporate actors who could compensate for the financial gap are acquiring more global powers by offering support in the form of their own platforms and technologies. This explains the phenomenon of such rapid growth for Google Arts & Culture (GAC) that in the past decade has transformed from a project sharing artefacts and street views of the seventeen top museums in the world, into a global heritage platform aggregating art collections, heritage sites, cultural traditions, natural wonders, and other forms of culture from more than eighty countries. GAC's geographical coverage and penetration is speedily spreading around the world, exemplifying the geopolitical strategy of Google and its *digital imperialism*. Digital heritage imperialism works via the political economy of domination and the monopolization of global media markets by powerful transnational corporations. For these global actors digital data is 'what oil and gas were for the beginning of the twentieth century', a key resource that fuels economic and political power (Powers and Jablonski, 2015: 75).

Employing the rhetoric of cultural access and democratization, and positioning GAC as corporate philanthropy, Google directly collaborates with major cultural institutions, governments, and even intergovernmental organizations, like UNESCO, to extract, digitize, and monopolize access to as much cultural data as possible, monetizing it in order to maximize its profits. This global hunt for data and user markets makes a corporate non-state economic actor a powerful geopolitical player, one with enough power, resources, and capabilities to compete with nation-states in the international arena. Unlike governments, for whom digital heritage aggregation is a process of politicization, shaped by national or supranational ideologies, the geopolitical agenda of Google, by contrast, boils down to its economic interests. This inevitably leads to the commodification of digital heritage, which raises public concerns about 'the erosion of public and publicly controlled cultural provision' of heritage resources and 'capital's systematic depletion of public culture' (Yeo, 2018).

The Future of Digital Heritage Aggregators: Navigating the Extremes

The case studies of digital heritage aggregation explored in this Element operate as both political and economically driven projects, but they all face similar issues of sustainability, particularly when their future development directly depends on the involved stakeholders' geopolitical interests and ambitions. Changes in these interests and shifts in geopolitical focus are accompanied by fluctuating funding priorities, which raise doubts about the ability of digital heritage aggregators to sustain their expensive infrastructures over time and serve their audiences. The four case studies offered a wide range of examples of aggregators' dependencies on their benefactors, which push them to different extremes on the scale of heritage instrumentalization: politicization or commodification.

The SMP portal demonstrates what happens when heritage aggregation unfolds under the strict control and patronage of a national government, leaving no space for the democratic participation of the public. Projects such as the SMP are doomed to failure, as their political values run counter to their social relevance to citizens, whose efforts in contributing their memories and heritage would inevitably decline if there were no political pressure or incentives to keep the collection growing. Since 2011, the SMP has become an abandoned digital cemetery, where a constructed memory-scape fails to communicate anything meaningful to the audience except banal nostalgia for urban spaces, transformed in the race for modernization, or a mere promotion of Singapore as a global hub to live in or visit and experience. Its closure in the near future signals the collapse of the geopolitics manifested in its digital heritage aggregation efforts, which solely rely on authoritarian will to secure digital sovereignty in the global environment. While other projects, like Trove and Europeana, do not necessarily raise the same degree of controversy, they mirror the foreign policy agendas and geopolitical dynamics of their stakeholders. This dependency casts a shadow on their genuine motivations and significantly affects how far public audiences can engage with the portals' materials, collections, exhibitions or campaigns as sites of (supra)national cultural, social and linguistic inclusion-exclusion.

The other extreme on the continuum of digital heritage instrumentalization is the example of Google, which in its pursuit of global heritage data and quest for new consumer markets, monetizes digital heritage through processes of exoticization, Disneyfication and commodification on the global scale. While there are no immediate threats to the project's economic vitality – it is clear that it serves Google to generate capital and it will continue to grow in line with this imperative – there are changing conditions that could undermine its bright future. For instance, in recent conversations with some Asian museums who joined GAC several years ago, it was revealed that not so many are willing to continue supplying Google with their digital materials. The limitations of the platform in terms of curatorial decision-making and its distortion of local, national, or regional representations which are hard to control on the institutional side, not to mention unresolved copyright issues, or the presentation of sacred heritage that requires differentiated access, are fundamental factors that put off many museums from collaborations with GAC.

Given these difficulties, in recent years Google has shifted the focus of its partnerships from museums to national governments, offering free services for digital place-making and nation-branding via the development of virtual tourism. Google Wonders projects is an illuminating example demonstrating a point where the interests of nation-states, especially those heavily dependent on tourist economies, converge with Google's global appetite for new heritage data and consumers, offering promising avenues for collaboration. However, with the economic rise of China and its rapid development in the digital domain, Google's project for planetary digital imperialism is under threat from other emerging actors. For example, in 2012 Baidu established Encyclopedia Digital Museum, which now operates up to 235 major online museums and cultural heritage sites in China and managed to establish collaborations with 400 Spanish museums, employing virtual AI, VR, and 3D technologies (Kaihao, 2018). Likewise, Chinese Alibaba, the world's largest e-commerce site, has partnered with several UK Museums and other prominent cultural institutions in Europe, providing its retailing platform Alifish to sell museums' products (Liu, 2016).

This competition for heritage aggregation is evidence that in the twenty-first century transnational capital, as a rising force in reconstituting cultural provisions, is a global phenomenon that significantly complicates relationships with and between (supra)national actors. The emergence of these new players in the digital global environment undermines 'the promise and peril of universal libraries' (Johns, 2018) and negates the possibility of establishing a truly 'encyclopedic museum' (Cuno, 2011), where all human knowledge and cultural heritage could collide to generate new wisdom, insight, and inspiration. Understanding the dangers surrounding the monopolization of heritage, in the hands of either a government or a corporation, this Element has started a conversation on the geopolitics of digital heritage, a field of study that is new in academic scholarship. The proliferation of the phenomenon of total digitization, as well as insights shared through the case studies, suggests that digital heritage geopolitics will continue to thrive as a research endeavour and will attract stronger attention from academics and cultural heritage specialists in years to come.

Perhaps finding a balance in the instrumentalization of digital heritage projects between corporate and state support and influence, as well as finding complementary avenues for heritage aggregators to sustain themselves and serve their audiences, should be the focus of future research. At the moment, the public is a constituency that is lacking agency in the geopolitical arena of digital heritage aggregation. Nor is there enough research on heritage platforms' audiences and communities, or an explicit articulation of how the digital public is constituted in aggregation projects. Future research should engage more closely with these issues to identify and document technologies of heritage geopolitical contestation, counter-movements, or sustainable open-source alternatives. As Dittmer and Bos suggest, we should not think of geopolitics 'as something "out there," far away from your everyday life', as 'the actions you take, and the way you respond to events, matter in terms of their geopolitical outcomes' (2019: 163). This Element has explored processes of digital heritage geopolitics, identifying and discussing aggregation on the global stage. The next step is to better understand if people's engagements with digital heritage aggregators can move beyond the consumption of imaginative geographies.

References

Abélès, M. (2000). Virtual Europe. In T. M. Wilson, and I. Bellier, eds., *An Anthropology of the European Union*. Oxford: Berg, pp. 31–52.

Abélès, M. (2004). Identity and Borders: An Anthropological Approach to EU Institutions. In *Twenty-First Century Papers: On-Line Working Papers from The Center for 21st Century Studies,* 1–26. https://minds.wisconsin.edu/handle/1793/28962

Adorno, T. W. (1982). *Prisms*. Cambridge, MA: The MIT Press.

Agnew, J. A. (2007). *Geopolitics: Re-visioning World Politics*. London: Routledge.

AIATSIS Website. (2022). Code of Ethics. https://aiatsis.gov.au/research/ethical-research/code-ethics.

Albinski, H., and Tow, W. (2002). ANZUS – Alive and Well after Fifty Years. *Australian Journal of Politics and History*, 48(2), 153–173.

Al-Rodhan, N. (2014). Meta-Geopolitics: The Relevance of Geopolitics in the Digital Age. *E-International Relations*. www.e-ir.info/2014/05/25/meta-geopolitics-the-relevance-of-geopolitics-in-the-digital-age/.

Amato, F., Martellozzo, F., Nolè, G., and Murgante, B. (2017). Preserving Cultural Heritage by Supporting Landscape Planning with Quantitative Predictions of Soil Consumption. *Journal of Cultural Heritage*, 23, 44–54. https://doi.org/10.1016/j.culher.2015.12.009.

Anderson, B. (1983). *Imagined Communities: Reflections on the Origin and Spread of Nationalism*. London: Verso.

Ang, I., Isar, Y. R., and Mar, P. (2015). Cultural Diplomacy: Beyond the National Interest? *International Journal of Cultural Policy*, 21(4), 365–381.

Ashworth, G. (1994). *Heritage, Tourism and Sustainability*. Tilburg: Tilburg University Press.

Ashworth, G. J., Graham, B. J., and Tunbridge, J. E. (2007). *Pluralising Pasts: Heritage, Identity and Place in Multicultural Societies*. London Pluto Press.

Aspinall, E. (2020). We Mustn't Allow Our National Library's Focus to Turn Inward. *The Canberra Times*, 30 May. www.canberratimes.com.au/story/6772932/we-mustnt-allow-our-national-librarys-focus-to-turn-inward/.

Aukia, J. (2019). Struggling for Recognition? Strategic Disrespect in China's Pursuit of Soft Power. *East Asia*, 36(4), 305–320.

Auletta, K. (2010). *Googled: The End of the World as We Know It*. London: Virgin.

Australian Government (AG). (2012). *Australia in the Asian Century.* White Paper. Canberra: Commonwealth of Australia. https://apo.org.au/sites/default/files/resource-files/2012-10/apo-nid31647.pdf.

Australian Library and Information Association (ALIA). (2018). Submission in Response to the Australian Government Soft Power Review. https://read.alia.org.au/alia-submission-response-australian-government-softpower-review-october-2018.

Ayres, M. L. (2013). 'Singing for their Supper': Trove, Australian Newspapers, and the Crowd. *ILFA WLIC Singapore*. https://library.ifla.org/id/eprint/245/1/153-ayres-en.pdf

Ayres, M. L. (2018). Unpublished Interview with Elizabeth Stainforth.

Badenoch, A. W. (2011). Harmonized Spaces, Dissonant Objects, Inventing Europe? Mobilizing Digital Heritage. *Culture Unbound*, 3, 295–315.

Barr, M. D., and Skrbiš, Z. (2011). *Constructing Singapore: Elitism, Ethnicity and the Nation-Building Project*. Copenhagen: Nias.

Bell, E. C. (2022). Understanding Soft Power Discourse in the National Library of Australia. *Journal of Documentation*, 78(6), 1457–1475.

Bendiek, A., Godehardt, N., and Schulze, D. (2019). The Age of Digital Geopolitics. *International Politics and Society Journal*. www.ips-journal.eu/in-focus/chinas-new-power/article/show/the-age-of-digital-geopolitics-3593/.

Bertrand M., and Kamenica E. (2018). *Coming Apart? Cultural Distances in the United States Over Time*. University of Chicago. www.nber.org/papers/w24771.

Bettivia, R., and Stainforth, E. (2019). The Dynamics of Scale in Digital Heritage Cultures. In T. Lähdesmäki, S. Thomas and Y. Zhu, eds., *Politics of Scale: New Directions in Critical Heritage Studies*. New York: Berghahn Books, pp. 50–62.

Bjola, C., and Holmes, M. (2015). *Digital Diplomacy: Theory and Practice*. Abingdon: Routledge.

Bjola, C., and Pamment, J. (2019). *Countering Online Propaganda and Extremism*. London: Routledge.

Björk, B., and Lundén, T. (2021). *Territory, State and Nation*. New York: Berghahn Books.

Blackburn, K. (2013). The 'Democratization' of Memories of Singapore's Past. *Bijdragen tot de Taal-, Land- en Volkenkunde*, 169(4), 431–456. https://doi.org/10.1163/22134379-12340064.

Blaschke, M. (2012). Explore Historic Sites with the World Wonders Project. https://blog.google/outreach-initiatives/arts-culture/explore-historic-sites-with-world/.

Bode, K. (2020). Why You Can't Model Away Bias. *Modern Language Quarterly*, 81(1).

Bogais, J., Garbuio, M., Groutsis, D. et al. (2022). Conquering 'The Tyranny of Distance': Australian–European Economic and Geopolitical Relationships Past, Present and Future. *European Management Journal*, 40(3), 310–319. https://doi.org/10.1016/j.emj.2022.02.003.

Bonacchi, C., and Krzyzanska, M. (2019). Digital Heritage Research Re-Theorised: Ontologies and Epistemologies in a World of Big Data. *International Journal of Heritage Studies*, 25(12), 1235–1247.

Bonde Thylstrup, N. (2018). *The Politics of Mass Digitization*. Cambridge, MA: MIT Press.

Borriello, A., and Brack, N. (2019). 'I Want My Sovereignty Back!': A Comparative Analysis of the Populist Discourses of Podemos, the 5 Star Movement, the FN and UKIP during the Economic and Migration Crises. *Journal of European Integration*, 41(7), 833–853.

Brew, C. (2019). Making Trove More Accessible. *National Film and Sound Archive Digital Directions, Canberra*. https://trove.nla.gov.au/sites/default/files/2019-12/Making%20Trove%20more%20accessible.pdf.

Brew, C. (2020). Trove Preview – What's the Same and What's Changed. *Trove Blog*. https://trove.nla.gov.au/blog/2020/01/29/trove-preview-whats-same-and-whats-changed.

Brown, D., and Nicholas, G. (2012). Protecting Indigenous Cultural Property in the Age of Digital Democracy: Institutional and Communal Responses to Canadian First Nations and Māori Heritage Concerns. *Journal of Material Culture*, 17(3), 307–324.

Bui, H., and Lee,T. (2015). Commodification and Politicization of Heritage: Implications for Heritage Tourism at the Imperial Citadel of Thang Long, Hanoi (Vietnam). *ASEAS – Austrian Journal of South-East Asian Studies*, 8(2), 187–202.

Byrne, D. (1996). Deep Nation: Australia's Acquisition of an Indigenous Past. *Aboriginal History*, 20, 82–107.

Caines, M. (2013). Arts head: Amit Sood, Director, Google Cultural Institute. *The Guardian*, 3 December. www.theguardian.com/culture-professionals-network/culture-professionals-blog/2013/dec/03/amit-sood-google-cultural-institute-art-project.

Calligaro, O. (2021). European Identity Between Culture and Values: From European Heritage to "Our European Way of Life". In F. Foret, and J. Vargovčíková, eds., *Value Politics in the European Union*. London: Routledge, pp. 133–150.

Cameron, F., and Kenderdine, S. (2007). *Theorizing Digital Cultural Heritage: A Critical Discourse*. Cambridge, MA: MIT Press.

Cameron, F., and Mengler, S. (2015). Transvisuality, Geopolitics and Cultural Heritage in Global Flows: The Israeli-Palestinian Conflict and The Death of the Virtual Terrorist. In T. Christensen, A. Michelsen, and F. Wiegand, eds., *Transvisuality: The Cultural Dimension of Visuality*, 2, pp. 59–72.

Campaign for Accountability (CFA). (2019). *Google's Diplomatic Edge*. Report. https://bit.ly/31XDbSb.

Candeloro, D. (2021). Digital Fashion Exhibition: Salvatore Ferragamo Museum and Google Arts & Culture. *Fashion Communication*, 129–142. https://doi.org/10.1007/978-3-030-81321-5_11.

Castells, M. (2008). The New Public Sphere: Global Civil Society, Communication Networks, and Global Governance. *The ANNALS of the American Academy of Political and Social Science*, 616(1), 78–93.

Caswell, M., Gabiola, J., Zavala, J., Brilmyer, G., and Cifor, M. (2018). Imagining Transformative Spaces: The Personal-Political Sites of Community Archives. *Archival Science*, 18, 73–93.

Caswell, M., Harter, C., and Bergis, J. (2017). Diversifying the Digital Historical Record: Integrating Community Archives in National Strategies for Access to Digital Cultural Heritage. *D-Lib Magazine*, 23(5–6). www.dlib.org/dlib/may17/caswell/05caswell.html

Cheney-Lippold, J. (2011). A New Algorithmic Identity: Soft Biopolitics and the Modulation of Control. *Theory, Culture and Society*, 28(6), 164–181.

Cheng, N. (2018). This is my Doodle: Non-Participation, Performance, and the Singapore Memory Project. *Performance Paradigm*. https://performanceparadigm.net/index.php/journal/article/view/213.

Chew, I., and Haliza, J. (2013). Preserving the Crowdsourced Memories of a Nation, The Singapore Memory Project. In L. Duranti and S. Elizabeth, eds., *The Memory of the World in the Digital Age: Digitization and Preservation*. Vancouver: UNESCO and The University of British Columbia, pp. 354–365.

Chong, A. (2010). Small State Soft Power Strategies: Virtual Enlargement in the Cases of the Vatican City State and Singapore. *Cambridge Review of International Affairs*, 23(3), 383–405. https://doi.org/10.1080/09557571.2010.484048.

Chong, T. (2005). Singapore's Cultural Policy and Its Consequences: From Global To Local. *Critical Asian Studies*, 37(4), 553–568.

Christen, K., Davis, L., Griffith, Z., and Neely, J. (2018). Traditional Knowledge and Digital Archives: An Interview with Kim Christen.

disClosure: A Journal of Social Theory, 27(5), 8–14. https://doi.org/10.13023/disclosure.27.02.

Chua, B. Ht. (2006). *Communitarian Ideology and Democracy in Singapore*. London: Routledge.

Ciolfi, L., Damala, A., Hornecker, E., Lechner, M., and Maye, L. (2017). *Cultural Heritage Communities*. London: Routledge.

Club 21. (n.d.). About Us. https://sg.club21global.com/club21/corporate_profile/.

Coe, P. (1994). The Struggle for Aboriginal Sovereignty. *Social Alternatives*, 13, 10–12.

Conti, G. (2009). *Googling Security: How Much Does Google Know about You?* Boston: Addison-Wesley.

Cook, T. (2013). Evidence, Memory, Identity, and Community: Four Shifting Archival Paradigms. *Archival Science*, 13, 95–120.

Coombe, R., and Weiss, L. (2015). Neoliberalism, Heritage Regimes, and Cultural Rights. In L. Meskell, ed., *Global Heritage: A Reader*. Chichester: Wiley Blackwell, pp. 43–69.

Cooper, M. (2015). Google Cultural Institute Puts Us All Onstage. *The New York Times*. 1 December. www.nytimes.com/2015/12/02/arts/music/google-cultural-institute-puts-us-all-onstage.html.

Cousins, J. (2017). Creating a Renaissance for the Library in the Digital Era. *Liber Quarterly*, 26(4), 260–272.

Cowin, J. (2020). Digital Worlds and Transformative Learning: Google Expeditions, Google Arts and Culture, and the Merge Cube. *International Research and Review*, 10(1), 42–53.

Culturebot website. (2022). About the Technology. https://culturebot.eu/.

Cuno, J. (2011). *Museums Matter*. Chicago: University of Chicago Press.

Curthoys, A. (1999). Expulsion, Exodus and Exile in White Australian Historical Mythology *Journal of Australian Studies*, 23(61), 1–19.

Curtin, P. A., and Gaither, T. K. (2007). *International Public Relations: Negotiating Culture, Identity, and Power*. Thousand Oaks: Sage Publications.

Dalbello, M. (2004). Institutional Shaping of Cultural Memory: Digital Library as Environment for Textual Transmission. *Library Quarterly*, 74(3), 265–298.

Dalbello, M. (2009). Cultural Dimensions of Digital Library Development, Part II: The Cultures of Innovation in Five European National Libraries (Narratives of Development). *Library Quarterly*, 79(1), 1–72.

Daley, B. (2021). Making Europeana Collections Multilingual. https://pro.europeana.eu/post/making-europeana-collections-multilingual.

Dallwitz, D., Dallwitz, J., and Lowish, S. (2019). A ra Irititja and A ra Winki in the APY Lands: Connecting Archives to Communities through Mobile Apps on Portable Devices. *Archives and Manuscripts*, 47(1), 35–52.

Davis, B. (2016). Google's Sprawling New Art App Has Grand Ambitions But Is Still Pretty Clunky. *Artnet News*. https://news.artnet.com/art-world/google-arts-culture-app-grand-ambitions-566183.

Davis, B. (2017). Google Disrupts Curating Via Artificial Intelligence. *Artnet News*. https://news.artnet.com/art-world/google-artificial-intelligence-812147.

De Largy Healy, J., and Glowczewski, B. (2016). Indigenous and Transnational Values in Oceania: Heritage Reappropriation, From Museums to the World Wide Web. *eTropic: Electronic Journal of Studies in the Tropics*, 13(2). https://doi.org/10.25120/etropic.13.2.2014.3313.

Delanty, G. (1995). *Inventing Europe: Idea, Identity, Reality*. London: Palgrave MacMillan.

Deng, M. (2020). Singapore as Non-Place: National Cinema Through the Lens of Temporal Heterogeneity. *Asian Cinema*, 31(1), 37–53. https://doi.org/10.1386/ac_00012_1.

Department of Foreign Affairs and Trade, Australia (DFAT). (2022a). United Kingdom Country Brief. www.dfat.gov.au/geo/united-kingdom/Pages/united-kingdom-country-brief.

Department of Foreign Affairs and Trade, Australia (DFAT). (2022b). China-Australia Free Trade Agreement. www.dfat.gov.au/trade/agreements/in-force/chafta/Pages/australia-china-fta.

Department of Home Affairs, Australia (DHA). (2022). Country Profiles. www.homeaffairs.gov.au/research-and-statistics/statistics/country-profiles/profiles.

Department of Infrastructure, Transport, Regional Development and Communications, Australia (DITRDCA). (2020). $8 Million to Enhance Australia's Trove Portal. www.arts.gov.au/departmental-news/8-million-enhance-australias-trove-portal.

Department of Infrastructure, Transport, Regional Development and Communications, Australia (DITRDCA). (2023). National Cultural Policy – Revive: A Place for Every Story, a Story for Every Place. www.arts.gov.au/publications/national-cultural-policy-revive-place-every-story-story-every-place.

Department of Statistics Singapore (DoSS). (2022). Environment. https://bit.ly/3pWJIKJ

De Cesari, C. (2013). Thinking Through Heritage Regimes. In R. F. Bendix, A. Eggert, and A. Peselmann, eds., *Heritage Regimes and the State*. Göttingen: Universitätsverlag Göttingen Press, pp. 399–413.

De Cesari, C. (2020). Heritage beyond the Nation-State? *Current Anthropology*, 61(1), 30–56. https://doi.org/10.1086/707208.

Di Blasio, M., and Di Blasio, R. (1983). Constructing a Cultural Context Through Museum Storytelling. *Roundtable Reports*, 8(3), 7–9.

Dijkink, G. (1998). Geopolitical Codes and Popular Representations. *GeoJournal*, 46(4), 293–299.

Dittmer, J., and Bos, D. (2019). *Popular Culture, Geopolitics, and Identity*. Lanham, Maryland: Rowman & Littlefield.

Dittmer, J., and Gray, N. (2010). Popular Geopolitics 2.0: Towards New Methodologies of the Everyday. *Geography Compass*, 4(11), 1664–1677.

Dodds, K., Kuus, M., and Sharp J. (2016). Introduction: Geopolitics and Its Critics. In K. Dodds, M. Kuus, and J. Sharp, eds., *The Ashgate Research Companion to Critical Geopolitics*. London: Routledge, pp. 1–14.

Dunin-Wąsowicz, R. (2015). *Culture for Europe: Struggles for Contemporary Meanings and Social Understandings of Europe through Cultural Institutions, Festivals, and Art Projects*. PhD Thesis, London School of Economics.

Dyson, G. (2012). *Turing's Cathedral: The Origins of the Digital Universe*. New York: Pantheon Books.

Edwards, A. (2010). What's Your Message? RunCoCo's Crowdsourcing Lessons from The Great War Archive. *RunCoCo Blog*. https://blogs.it.ox.ac.uk/runcoco/2010/09/24/whats-your-message/.

Elad, S. (2010). *Google and the Digital Divide: The Bias of Online Knowledge*. Oxford: Chandos.

Erway, R. (2009). A View on Europeana from the US Perspective. *Liber Quarterly*, 19(2), 103–121.

Europa. (2010). i2010 strategy for an Innovative and Inclusive European Information Society. http://ec.europa.eu/information_society/doc/factsheets/035-i2010-en.pdf.

Europa. (2018). New European Agenda for Culture. https://culture.ec.europa.eu/policies/strategic-framework-for-the-eus-cultural-policy.

Europa. (2022). EU Motto. https://european-union.europa.eu/principles-countries-history/symbols/eu-motto_en.

European Commission (EC). (2016). Joint Communication to the European Parliament and the Council, Towards an EU Strategy for International Cultural Relations. https://eurlex.europa.eu/legal-content/EN/TXT/?uri=JOIN%3A2016%3A29%3AFIN.

European Commission (EC). (2021a). EC Recommendation on a Common European Data Space for Cultural Heritage. https://eur-lex.europa.eu/legal-content/EN/TXT/?uri=CELEX:32021H1970.

European Commission (EC). (2021b). The Digital Europe Programme 2021–2022. https://digital-strategy.ec.europa.eu/en/activities/work-programmes-digital.

Europeana. (2011). Strategic Plan 2011–2015. https://pro.europeana.eu/files/Europeana_Professional/Publications/Strategic%20Plan%202011–2015%20%28colour%29.pdf.

Europeana. (2014). Europeana Strategy 2015–2020. http://pro.europeana.eu/files/Europeana_Professional/Publications/Europeana%20Strategy%202020.pdf.

Europeana. (2020). Strategic Plan 2020–2025. https://pro.europeana.eu/files/Europeana_Professional/Publications/EU2020StrategyDigital_May2020.pdf.

Europeana Conference (EC). (2022). Culture & Tourism: From a Project Case Study Toward Data Spaces Synergies. https://youtu.be/YjQqPV8CEjM.

Europeana Storytelling Task Force (ESTF). (2021). Europeana as a Powerful Platform for Storytelling: Report and Recommendations. https://pro.europeana.eu/project/europeana-as-a-powerful-platform-for-storytelling.

Evans, J. (2018). Unpublished Interview with Elizabeth Stainforth.

Evans, J., and Wilson, J. Z. (2018). Inclusive Archives and Recordkeeping: Towards a Critical Manifesto. *International Journal of Heritage Studies*, 24(8), 857–860.

Fiott, D. (2021). In Search of Meaning and Action. In D. Fiott, ed., *European Sovereignty: Strategy and Interdependence*. Paris: European Union Institute for Security Studies. Chaillot Paper, 169, 4–6.

flickr. (2022). PictureAustralia Australia Day Group to Close After 20 November. *Trove: Australia in Pictures*. www.flickr.com/groups/pictureaustralia_ppe/discuss/72157594353310827/.

Flinn, A., Stevens, M., and Shepherd, E. (2009). Whose Memories, Whose Archives? Independent Community Archives, Autonomy, and the Mainstream. *Archival Science*, 9, 71–86.

Flint, C. (2017). *Introduction to Geopolitics*. 3rd ed. London: Routledge.

Flint, C. (2022). Putting the 'Geo' into Geopolitics: A Heuristic Framework and the Example of Australian Foreign Policy. *GeoJournal*, 87(4), 2577–2592.

Foo, S., Tang, C., and Ng, J. (2010). Libraries for Life: A Case Study of National Library Board, Singapore. *International Conference commemorating the 40th Anniversary of the Korean Society for Library and Information Science*, Seoul, Korea, October 8.

Foreign Policy (FP). (2019). FP's Diplomat of the Year. *Foreign Policy*. https://foreignpolicy.com/fp-diplomat-of-the-year/.

Foucault, M. (1991). Governmentality. In G. Burchell, C. Gordon, and P. Miller, eds., *The Foucault Effect: Studies in Governmentality*. London: Wheatsheaf Harvester, pp. 87–104.

Foucault, M. (2002). *Archaeology of Knowledge*. Trans. A. M. Sheridan Smith. London: Routledge.

Freire, N., Meijers, E., Voorburg, R., and Isaac, A. (2018). Aggregation of Cultural Heritage Datasets through the Web of Data. *Procedia Computer Science*, 137, 120–126. https://doi.org/10.1016/j.procs.2018.09.012.

Gajardo, T., and Lau, Y. (2017). The Woman Who is Bringing Museums & Cultural Sites from All Over the World to your fingertips. *The Artling*, March 15. https://theartling.com/en/artzine/interview-head-google-arts-culture-suhair-khan/.

Gibson, C. (1999). Cartographies of the Colonial and Capitalist State: A Geopolitics of Indigenous Self-determination in Australia. *Antipode*, 31, 45–79.

Gibson, C. (2016). Indigenous Geopolitics. In K. Dodds, M. Kuus, and J. Sharp, eds., *The Ashgate Research Companion to Critical Geopolitics*. London: Routledge, pp. 421–438.

Gibson, W. (1993). Disneyland with the Death Penalty. *Wired*. www.wired.com/1993/04/gibson-2/.

Gillespie, T. (2014). The Relevance of Algorithms. In T. Gillespie, P. Boczkowski, and K. Foot, eds., *Media Technologies*. Cambridge, MA: MIT Press, pp. 167–194.

Glovine, A. M. (2008). *The Heritage-Scape: UNESCO, World Heritage, and Tourism*. Lanham: Lexington Books.

Goh, D. P. S. (2013). Walking the Global City. *Space and Culture*, 17(1), 16–28. https://doi.org/10.1177/1206331212451686.

Gomez, J. (2000). *Self Censorship: Singapore's Shame*. Singapore: Think Centre.

Google Arts & Culture (GAC). (2022a). Partners. https://about.artsandculture.google.com/partners/.

Google Arts & Culture (GAC). (2022b). About. https://about.artsandculture.google.com/partners/.

Google Arts & Culture (GAC). (2022c). Arts & Culture Experiments. https://experiments.withgoogle.com/collection/arts-culture.

Google Arts & Culture (GAC). (2022d). Wonders of Vietnam. https://artsandculture.google.com/project/wonders-of-vietnam.

Google Arts & Culture (GAC). (2023). World Wonders. https://artsandculture.google.com/project/explore-world-heritage.

Google. (2022a). Our Offices. https://about.google/locations.

Google. (2022b). Google Data Centers. www.google.com/about/datacenters/locations/.

Google. (2022c). Cloud Locations. https://cloud.google.com/about/locations#network.

Gramer, R. (2017). Denmark Creates the World's First Ever Digital Ambassador. *Foreign Policy*. https://foreignpolicy.com/2017/01/27/denmark-creates-the-worlds-first-ever-digital-ambassador-technology-europe-diplomacy/.

Grau, D. (2021). *Under Discussion: The Encyclopedic Museum*. Los Angeles, CA: Getty Research Institute.

Gray, J. E. (2020). *Google Rules: The History and Future of Copyright under the Influence of Google*. New York: Oxford University Press.

Grincheva, N. (2012). Canada's Got Treasures! Constructing National Identity through Cultural Participation. In S. Austen, Z. Bishop, K. Deventer, R. Lala, and M. Ramos, eds., *The Cultural Component of Citizenship*. Brussels: European House for Culture, pp. 79–99.

Grincheva, N. (2019). The Form and Content of 'Digital Spatiality': Mapping the Soft Power of DreamWorks Animation in Asia. *Asiascape: Digital Asia*, 6(1), 58–83.

Grincheva, N. (2020). *Museum Diplomacy in the Digital Age*. London: Routledge.

Gustin, S. (2013). Google Unveils Tools to Access Web from Repressive Countries. *The Business Times*. 21 October. https://business.time.com/2013/10/21/google-digital-rebels/.

Hall, S. (1992). The West and the Rest: Discourse and Power. In S. Hall, and B. Gieben, eds., *Formations of Modernity*. Cambridge, MA: Polity Press in association with the Open University, pp. 185–227.

Hall, S. (1999). Un-Settling 'The Heritage', Re-Imagining the Post-Nation. Whose Heritage? *Third Text*, 13(49), 3–13.

Harrison, R. (2012). *Heritage: Critical Approaches*. London: Routledge.

Harvey, D.C. (2001). Heritage Pasts and Heritage Presents: temporality, meaning and the scope of heritage studies. International Journal of Heritage Studies, 7(4), 319–138.

Heng, D., Thiam, S., and Aljunied, S. M. (2009). *Reframing Singapore: Memory, Identity, Trans-Regionalism*. Amsterdam: Amsterdam University Press.

Herwitz, D. (2012). *Heritage, Culture, and Politics in the Postcolony*. NYC: Columbia University Press.

Higgott, R. (2020). EU Cultural Diplomacy: A Contextual Analysis of Constraints and Opportunities. In C. Carta, and R. Higgott, eds., *Cultural Diplomacy in Europe: Between the Domestic and the International*. London, Cham: Palgrave Macmillan, pp. 19–40.

Hill, M., and Kwen, F. L. (2016). *The Politics of Nation Building and Citizenship in Singapore*. London: Routledge.

Hillis, K., Petit, M., and Jarrett, K. (2012). *Google and the Culture of Search*. New York: Routledge.

Hobsbawm, E., and Ranger, T. (1992). *The Invention of Tradition*. Cambridge: Cambridge University Press.

Holley, H. (2011). Trove: Innovation in Access to Information in Australia *Ariadne*, 64. www.ariadne.ac.uk/issue64/holley/.

Hooton, F. (2006). PictureAustralia and the flickr Effect *NLA Gateways*, 80. https://webarchive.nla.gov.au/awa/20060529045055/http://pandora.nla.gov.au/pan/11779/20060524-0000/www.nla.gov.au/pub/gateways/issues/80/story01.html.

Hooton, F. (2007). Democratising History: Evaluating PictureAustralia's flickr Pilot Project. *NLA Gateways*, 84. https://webarchive.nla.gov.au/awa/20070525063525/http://pandora.nla.gov.au/pan/11779/20070524-0000/www.nla.gov.au/pub/gateways/issues/84/story13.html.

Hulsman, J. C. (2019). Digital Geopolitics and Political Risk. *Aspenia Online*. https://aspeniaonline.it/digital-geopolitics-and-political-risk/.

Hunt, W. A. (2010). Google's Foreign Policy: And a Wider East/West Geopolitical Shift. *The International Journal of Science in Society*, 1(4), 105–114. https://doi.org/10.18848/1836-6236/cgp/v01i04/51507.

Isaac, A. (2013). Europeana Data Model Primer. https://pro.europeana.eu/files/Europeana_Professional/Share_your_data/Technical_requirements/EDM_Documentation/EDM_Primer_130714.pdf.

Ismail, F. (2013). Real History is Written in People's Everyday Lives. *New Straits Times*, 26 March. http://www.nst.com.my/nation/general/real-history-is-written-in-people-s-everyday-lives-1.241799.

Jeanneney, J. (2007). *Google and the Myth of Universal Knowledge: A View from Europe*. Chicago: University of Chicago Press.

Jiang, M. (2013). The Business and Politics of Search Engines: A Comparative Study of Baidu and Google's Search Results of Internet Events in China. *New Media & Society*, 16(2), 212–233. https://doi.org/10.1177/1461444813481196.

Jin, D. Y. (2017). *Digital Platforms, Imperialism and Political Culture*. New York: Routledge.

Jin, T. (2022). Virtual Wonders: Google Arts & Culture Makes Art Accessible to All. *AmCham China*. www.amchamchina.org/virtual-wonders-google-arts-culture-makes-art-accessible-to-all/.

Johns, A. (2018). The Promise and Peril of Universal Libraries. www.abaa.org/member-articles/the-promise-and-peril-of-universal-libraries.

Johnston, C. (2021). A Pathway to Intangible Cultural Heritage Protection?: Examining the Victorian Legislation in the context of Australian Heritage Practice *Historic Environment*, 33(1/2), 62–80.

Kaihao, W. (2018). Spanish Pilgrimage Route Soon in Baidu Encyclopedia. *China Daily*. www.chinadailyhk.com/articles/228/66/156/1518064537773.html.

Kalay, Y. E., Kvan, T., and Affleck, J. (2007). *New Heritage: New Media and Cultural Heritage*. London: Routledge.

Kaplan, R. (2012). *The Revenge of Geography: What The Map Tells Us About Coming Conflicts and the Battle Against Fate*. NYC: Random House.

Kathiravelu, L. (2017). Rethinking Race: Beyond the CMIO Categorisations. *Dr.ntu.edu.sg*. https://hdl.handle.net/10356/152310.

Kawasaki, K. (2004). Cultural Hegemony of Singapore among ASEAN Countries: Globalization and Cultural Policy. *International Journal of Japanese Sociology*, 13(1), 22–35. https://doi.org/10.1111/j.1475-6781.2004.00051.x.

Kelley, R. (2014). *Agency Change: Diplomatic Action Beyond the State*. Lanham: Rowman & Littlefield.

Kersel, M., and Luke, C. (2015). Civil Societies? Heritage Diplomacy and Neo-Imperialism. In L. Meskell, ed., *Global Heritage: A Reader*. Chichester: Wiley Blackwell, pp. 70–93.

King, R. (2008). *The Singapore Miracle, Myth and Reality*. Inglewood, WA: Insight Press.

Kizhner, I., Terras, M., Rumyantsev, M. et al. (2021). Digital Cultural Colonialism: Measuring Bias in Aggregated Digitized Content Held in Google Arts and Culture. *Digital Scholarship in the Humanities*, 36(3), 607–640.

Kizhner, I., Terras, M., Rumyantsev, M., Sycheva, K., and Rudov, I. (2018). Accessing Russian Culture Online: The Scope of Digitization in Museums Across Russia. *Digital Scholarship in the Humanities*, 34(2), 350–367. https://doi.org/10.1093/llc/fqy035.

Knutsen, T. L. (2014). Halford J. Mackinder, Geopolitics, and the Heartland Thesis. *The International History Review*, 36(5), 835–857. www.jstor.org/stable/24703263.

Labadi, S. (2005). A Review of the Global Strategy for a Balanced, Representative and Credible World Heritage List 1994–2004. *Conservation and Management of Archaeological Sites*,7, 89–102.

Lähdesmäki, T. (2014). The EU's Explicit and Implicit Heritage Politics *European Societies*, 16(3), 401–421.

Lähdesmäki, T., Čeginskas, V. L., Kaasik-Krogerus, S., Mäkinen, K., and Turunen, J. (2020). *Creating and Governing Cultural Heritage in the European Union: The European Heritage Label*. London: Routledge.

Lähdesmäki, T., Suzie, T., and Zhu, J. (eds.) (2019). *Politics of Scale*. New York: Berghahn Books.

Larson, C. (2010). State Department Innovator Goes to Google. *Foreign Policy*, 7 September. https://foreignpolicy.com/2010/09/07/state-department-innovator-goes-to-google/.

Li, J., He, L., Sung, H. and Shengnan, M. (2014). *Forbidden City: Imperial Treasures from the Palace Museum, Beijing*. Richmond: Virginia Museum of Fine Arts.

Lee, H. L. (2011). PMO | National Day Rally 2011. *Prime Minister's Office Singapore*. 21 August 2019. https://bit.ly/3AYv3EZ.

Lee, T. (2004). Popularising Policy: (Re)forming Culture and the Nation in Singapore. *Asia Pacific Journal of Arts and Cultural Management*, 2(1), 55–69.

Lee, T. (2012). *The Media, Cultural Control and Government in Singapore*. London: Routledge.

Lee, W. (2014). Amit Sood, founder of Google Art Project, talks about how technology changes experience of viewing art. *Herald Interview*, 22 September.

Lévy, M., Niggemann, E., and De Decker, J. (2011). *The New Renaissance, Report of the Comité des Sages on Bringing Europe's Cultural Heritage Online*. Brussels: Publications Office. https://data.europa.eu/doi/10.2759/45571.

Lewi, H., Smith, W., Vom Lehn, D., and Cooke, S. eds. (2020). *The Routledge International Handbook of New Digital Practices in Galleries, Libraries, Archives, Museums and Heritage Sites*. Abingdon: Routledge.

Li, J., Sun, C., Xanat, V. M., and Ochiai, Y. (2022). Electroencephalography and Self-Assessment Evaluation of Engagement with Online Exhibitions: Case Study of Google Arts and Culture *Culture and Computing*, 316–331. https://doi.org/10.1007/978-3-031-05434-1_21.

Li, S., and Womack, B. (2012). Google China Business Grows, 'Continues to Thrive', Alegre Says. *Bloomberg*, 24 January. www.bloomberg.com/news/articles/2012-01-24/google-china-business-grows-continues-to-thrive-alegre-says#xj4y7vzkg.

Liaropoulos, A. (2021). EU Digital Sovereignty: A Regulatory Power Searching for Its Strategic Autonomy in the Digital Domain. In *Proceedings of the 20th European Conference on Cyber Warfare and Security*.24–25 June.

Liew, K. K., and Pang, N. (2015). Fuming and Fogging Memories: Civil Society and State in Communication of Heritage in Singapore in the Cases of the Singapore Memories Project and the 'Marxist Conspiracy' of 1987. *Continuum*, 29(4), 549–60. https://doi.org/10.1080/10304312.2015.1051806.

Liew, K. K., Pang, N., and Chan, B. (2014). Industrial Railroad to Digital Memory Routes: Remembering the Last Railway in Singapore. *Media, Culture & Society*, 36(6), 761–75. https://doi.org/10.1177/0163443714532984.

Liu, C. (2016). Alibaba Helps Sell British Museum Products. *China Daily*. www.chinadaily.com.cn/world/2016-11/02/content_27255172.html.

Macdonald, M. (2013). *Memorylands: Heritage and Identity in Europe Today*. London: Routledge.

Macmillan, F. (2017). Heritage, Imperialism and Commodification: How the West Can Always Do It Best. *Europa Ethnica*, 74(3–4), 114–124. https://doi.org/10.24989/0014-2492-2017-34-114.

MacroTrends (MT). (2022). Vietnam Tourism Statistics 2003–2022. www.macrotrends.net/countries/VNM/vietnam/tourism-statistics.

Madiega, T. (2020). *Digital Sovereignty for Europe* (Briefing PE 651.992; EPRS Ideas Papers). European Parliamentary Research Service. www.europarl.europa.eu/RegData/etudes/BRIE/2020/651992/EPRS_BRI(2020)651992_EN.pdf.

Malpas, J. (2007). Cultural Heritage in the Age of New Media. In Y. E. Kalay, T. Kvan, and J. Affleck, eds., *New heritage: New Media and Cultural Heritage*. London: Routledge, pp. 13–26.

Mankekar, P. (1999). *Screening Culture, Viewing Politics: An Ethnography of Television, Womanhood, and Nation in Postcolonial India*. Durham, NC: Duke University

Mann, D. (2018). Unpublished Interview with Elizabeth Stainforth.

Manners, I. (2002). 'Normative Power Europe: A Contradiction in Terms?'. *Journal of Common Market Studies*, 40(2), 235–258.

Manners, I., and Diez, T. (2007). Reflecting on Normative Power Europe. In F. Berenskoetter, and M. J. Williams, eds., *Power in World Politics*. New York: Routledge, pp. 173–188.

Mansfield, E. C. (2014). Google Art Project and Digital Scholarship in the Visual Arts. *Visual Resources: An International Journal of Documentation*, 30(1), 110–17.

Marton, A. (2011). *Forgotten as Data – Remembered through Information. Social Memory Institutions in the Digital Age: The Case of the Europeana Initiative*. PhD Thesis, London School of Economics

McCarthy, D. (2022). Presentation at Data To Power Webinar: GLAM Collections and Exhibitions in Immersive Environments. www.youtube.com/watch?v=VH-Kn5hGabw&t=3689s.

McCrary, Q. (2011). The Political Nature of Digital Cultural Heritage. *LIBER Quarterly*, 20(3–4), 357–368.

McDonald, M. (1996). 'Unity in Diversity': Some Tensions in the Construction of Europe. *Social Anthropology*, 4, 47–60.

Medcalf, R. (2020). *Indo-Pacific Empire: China, America, and the Contest for the World's Pivotal Region*. Manchester: Manchester University Press.

Medeiros, B. (2021). 'There's No Way Abraham Lincoln Could Work at Google': Fox News and the Politics of Breaking Up Big Tech. *Journal of Communication Inquiry*, 46(1), 39–59. https://doi.org/10.1177/01968599211039211.

Meskell, L., and Brumann, C. (2015). UNESCO and New World Orders. In L. Meskell, ed. *Global Heritage: A Reader*. Chichester: Wiley Blackwell, pp. 22–42.

Metakides, G. (2022). A Crucial Decade for European Digital Sovereignty. In H. Werthner, E. Prem, E. A. Lee, and C. Ghezzi, eds., *Perspectives on Digital Humanism*. Cham: Springer International, pp. 219–226.

Mignolo, W. D. (2002). The Geopolitics of Knowledge and the Colonial Difference. *The South Atlantic Quarterly*, 101(1), 57–96.

Miller, R., Ruru, J., Behrendt, L., and Lindberg, T. (2012). *Discovering Indigenous Lands*. Oxford: Oxford University Press.

Ministry of Culture, Community, and Youth (MCCY). (2013). *The Report of the Arts and Culture Strategic Review, Singapore*. https://bit.ly/3TwSFIn.

Mirrlees, T. (2013). *Global Entertainment Media: Between Cultural Imperialism and Cultural Globalization*. London: Routledge.

National Gallery Singapore Representative (NGSR). (2023). Interview by Grincheva. February 2023.

National Heritage Board (NHB). (2008). *Renaissance City Plan III: Heritage Development Plan*. NHB: Singapore.

National Heritage Board (NHB). (2010). Singapore's Heritage and Museums Go Virtual with a Package of Online Initiatives. *NHB's Overall E-engagement Strategy*. Singapore: NHB.

National Library Board (NLB). (2023). E-mail Interview by Natalia Grincheva, 27 February 2023.

National Library of Australia (NLA). (2009). New Directions 2009–2011. www.nla.gov.au/library/NLA_Directions_2009-2011.pdf.

National Library of Australia (NLA). (2020a). Collection Development Policy. www.nla.gov.au/sites/default/files/collection_development_policy_revised_2_july.pdf

National Library of Australia (NLA). (2020b). Annual Report 2019–2020. www.nla.gov.au/sites/default/files/national_library_of_australia_annual_report_2019-20.pdf.

National Library of Australia (NLA). (2021). Trove Strategy 2021–2023. www.nla.gov.au/sites/default/files/2022-10/Trove%20Strategy_1.pdf.

National Library of Australia (NLA). (2022). Annual Report 2021–2022. www.nla.gov.au/sites/default/files/2022-10/NLA%20AR%202021–22%20Web.pdf.

Neale, M. (2017). The Third Archive and Artist as Archivist. In D. Jorgensen, and I. Mclean, eds., *Indigenous Archives: The Making and Unmaking of Aboriginal Art*. Perth: University of Western Australia Press, pp. 269–294.

Neumann, K. (2019). In Search of 'Australia and the Australian People': The National Library of Australia and the Representation of Cultural and Linguistic Diversity. In K. Darian-Smith, and P. Hamilton, eds., *Remembering Migration: Oral Histories and Heritage in Australia*. Cham: Palgrave Macmillan, pp. 285–299.

Ng, E. (2011). The Library as an Online Community Touch-Point. *IFLA World Library and Information Congress*, San Juan, Puerto Rico, 13–18 August.

NLA Website. (2022). National Library of Australia 2030. www.nla.gov.au/content/national-library-of-australia-2030

Nye, J. S. (1990). *Bound to Lead: The Changing Nature of American Power.* New York: Basic Books.

Nye, J. S. (1999). Redefining the National Interest. *Foreign Affairs*, 78(4), 22–35.

Nye, J. S. (2004). *Soft Power: The Means to Success in World Politics*. New Delhi: Knowledge World.

Ó Tuathail, G., and Agnew, J. (1992). Geopolitics and Discourse: Practical Geopolitical Reasoning in American Foreign Policy. *Political Geography*, 11(2), 190–204. https://doi.org/10.1016/0962-6298(92)90048-x.

Ó Tuathail, G. (1999). Understanding Critical Geopolitics: Geopolitics and Risk Society. *The Journal of Strategic Studies*, 22(2–3), 107–124.

Ó Tuathail, G. (2005). *Critical Geopolitics: The Politics of Writing Global Space*. London: Taylor & Francis.

Parkinson, G. (2020). Will Technology End the English Language's Global Domination? https://newseu.cgtn.com/news/2020-12-26/Will-technology-end-the-English-language-s-global-domination–WfQn5ByAKI/index.html.

Parry, R. (2007). *Recoding the Museum: Digital Heritage and the Technologies of Change*. London: Routledge.

Parry, R. (ed.) (2010). *Museums in a Digital Age*. Abingdon: Routledge.

Pascoal, S., Tallone, L., and Furtado, M. (2019). Cultural Tourism: Using Google Arts & Culture Platform to Promote a Small City in the North of Portugal. *Advances in Tourism, Technology and Smart Systems*, 171, 47–56. https://doi.org/10.1007/978-981-15-2024-2_5.

Passerini, L. ed. (1998). *The Question of European Identity: A Cultural Historical Approach*. Florence: European Historical Institute.

Pearson, L. (2017). Opinion: Invasion Day, Survival Day, or Day of Mourning? All of the Above. *Special Broadcasting Service*. www.sbs.com.au/nitv/article/opinion-invasion-day-survival-day-or-day-of-mourning-all-of-the-above/4iundmt2r.

Peter-Agbia, P. (2022). Bringing Art to the Streets with Pop Legends BTS. https://blog.google/outreach-initiatives/arts-culture/bringing-art-to-the-streets-with-pop-legends-bts/.

Pin, W. W. (2013). Interview by Natalia Grincheva, May 5.

Pin, W. W. (2014). Memory and the Nation: On the Singapore Memory Project. *Alexandria: The Journal of National and International Library and Information Issues*, 25(3), pp. 63–70. https://doi.org/10.7227/alx.0031.

Poole, N. (2014). Unpublished Interview with Elizabeth Stainforth.

Potter, E. (2002). *Cyber-Diplomacy: Managing Foreign Policy in the Twenty-First Century*. Montreal, QC: McGill-Queen's Press.

Povroznik, N. (2018). Towards a Global Infrastructure for Digital Cultural Heritage. In *Digital Heritage. Progress in Cultural Heritage: Documentation, Preservation, and Protection*. EuroMed, vol. 11196. Cham: Springer, pp. 607–615. https://doi.org/10.1007/978-3-030-01762-0_53.

Powers, S. M., and Jablonski, M. (2015). *The Real Cyber war: The Political Economy of Internet Freedom*. Urbana: University Of Illinois Press.

Public Service Division (PSD). (n.d.). Cultivating a Harmonious society, Becoming One People. www.psd.gov.sg/heartofpublicservice/our-institutions/cultivating-a-harmonious-society-becoming-one-people/.

Punathambekarm A., and Mohan, S. (2019). *Global Digital Cultures: Perspectives from South Asia*. Ann Arbor: University of Michigan Press.

Quang, T., William, N., and Paulson, D. (2022). Rising Tensions: Heritage-Tourism Development and the Commodification of 'Authentic' Culture among the Cham Community of Vietnam. *Cogent Social Sciences*, 8(1), 1–23. https://doi.org/10.1080/23311886.2022.2116161.

Rahman, F. (2020). The Intersection of Emergent Technologies and Geopolitics: Implications for Singapore. *S. Rajaratnam School of International Studies*. www.jstor.org/stable/resrep24284#metadata_info_tab_contents.

Regional Coordinator Asia (RCA). (2022). Interview by Natalia Grincheva. November 2022.

Remaking Singapore Committee (RSC). (2003). *Changing Mindsets, Deepening Relationships: The Report of the Remaking Singapore Committee*. Singapore: Government of Singapore.

Richey, S., and Taylor, J. B. (2017). *Google and Democracy.* London: Routledge.

Ronfeldt, D., and Arquilla, J. (1999). *The Emergence of Noopolitik: Toward an American Information Strategy.* Santa Monica, CA: Rand Corporation.

Ronfeldt, D., and Arquilla, J. (2020). Noopolitik: A New Paradigm for Public Diplomacy. In N. Snow, and N. Cull, eds., *Routledge Handbook of Public Diplomacy.* London: Routledge, pp. 445–480.

Ross, M. (2022). Oh, the Places You Will (Virtually) Go. *The Mercury News.* www.mercurynews.com/2022/07/21/oh-the-places-you-will-go-courtesy-of-google-arts-and-culture/.

Roy, D. (1994). Singapore, China, and the 'Soft Authoritarian' Challenge. *Asian Survey*, 34(3), 231–242. https://doi.org/10.2307/2644982.

Said, E. W. (1978). *Orientalism*. NYC: Pantheon Books.

Saran, S. (2020). Navigating the Digitisation of Geopolitics, *ORF.* www.orfonline.org/expert-speak/navigating-the-digitisation-of-geopolitics-60612/.

Sharma, K. (2017). High Culture has Been Under Lock and Key, says Google's Amit Sood. *mint.* www.livemint.com/Companies/xERUCxIqSLD9Z2zmUpWVOL/High-culture-has-been-under-lock-and-key-says-Google-Cultur.html.

Shepherd, R. (2006). UNESCO and the Politics of Cultural Heritage in Tibet. *Journal of Contemporary Asia*, 36(2), 243–257. https://doi.org/10.1080/00472330680000141.

Sherratt, T. (2016). Hacking Heritage: Power and Participation in Digital Cultural Collections. *2016 Digital GLAM Symposium.* http://discontents.com.au/hacking-heritage-power-and-participation-in-digital-cultural-collections/index.html.

Sherratt, T. (2019). Trove: Connecting Us to the Past. https://timsherratt.org/blog/trove-connecting-us/.

Shiva, V. (1993). Monocultures of the Mind. *Trumpeter*, 10(4), 2–11.

Shore, C. (2000). *Building Europe: The Cultural Politics of European Integration*. London: Routledge.

Shore, C. (2006). 'In Uno Plures' (?) EU Cultural Policy and the Governance of Europe. *Cultural Analysis*, 5, 7–26.

Singapore 21 Committee (S21C). (2001). Singapore 21: Together, We Make the Difference. Singapore: Singapore 21 Committee. https://www.nlb.gov.sg/main/article-detail?cmsuuid=66f2445b-43c1-407a-a3e8-a89083d6f868.

Singapore Memory Portal (SMP). (2015). SG Heart Map. www.singaporememory.sg/campaigns/sg-heart-map?nextrecord=9&listtype=campaigns&id=115&campaign=sg-heart-map.

Singapore Memory Portal (SMP). (n.d.). Help & Information, Singapore Memory. www.singaporememory.sg/Help-Info.

Singapore Tourism Board (STB). (2000). *Official Guide: Singapore New Asia*. Singapore: Singapore Tourism Board.

SimilarWeb (SW). (2022). Google Arts and Culture Statistics. www.similarweb.com/website/artsandculture.google.com/#overview.

Singapore Tourist Promotion Board, & Ministry of Information and the Arts (STPB & MIA). (1995). Singapore, Global City for the Arts. Joint report.

Smith, L. (2006). *Uses of Heritage*. London: Routledge.

Sood, A. (2015). Step on Stage with the Google Cultural Institute. *Google Official Blog: Arts & Culture*. https://blog.google/outreach-initiatives/arts-culture/step-on-stage-with-google-cultural/.

Sood, A. (2022). Techies are the New Artists, Says Google Art Czar Amit Sood. *The Times of India*, 10 August. https://timesofindia.indiatimes.com/business/india-business/techies-are-the-new-artists-says-google-art-czar-amit-sood/articleshow/93468078.cms?utm_source=contentofinterest&utm_medium=text&utm_campaign=cppst.

StatCounter Global Stats (SC). (2022). Search Engine Market Share China 2019. https://gs.statcounter.com/search-engine-market-share/all/china.

StatCounter (SC). (2022). Search Engine Market Share China | StatCounter Global Stats. https://gs.statcounter.com/search-engine-market-share/all/china.

Statista. (2022). Search Engine Market Share Worldwide | Statista. [online] Statista.www.statista.com/statistics/216573/worldwide-market-share-of-search-engines/.

Statistics Singapore (SS). (2023). Population in Brief. Report.www.population.gov.sg/files/media-centre/publications/population-in-brief-2023.pdf.

Stiegler, B. (2010). Telecracy against Democracy. *Cultural Politics*, 6, 171–180.

Susan, L., and Brian, W. (2012). Google China Business Grows, 'Continues to Thrive', Alegre Says. *Bloomberg*, 24 January. www.bloomberg.com/news/articles/2012-01-24/google-china-business-grows-continues-to-thrive-alegre-says.

Tan, G. (2012). Giving the Past a Present: The Singapore Memory Project. *International Conference on New Media, Memories and Histories*, 5–6 October 2012, Wee Kim Wee School of Communication.

Tan, G. (2013). Interview by Natalia Grincheva, 5 May.

Tan, K. P. (2016). Choosing What to Remember in Neoliberal Singapore: The Singapore Story, State Censorship and State-Sponsored Nostalgia. *Asian Studies Review*, 40(2), 231–249. https://doi.org/10.1080/10357823.2016.1158779.

Tang, C. (2013). Acquiring, Organising and Providing Access to Digital Content: The Singapore Memory Project Experience. Paper presented at the *IFLA World Library and Information Congress*, Singapore, Future Libraries: Infinite Possibilities Singapore. https://library.ifla.org/id/eprint/214/1/198-tang-en.pdf.

Taylor, J., and Gibson, L. K. (2017). Digitisation, Digital Interaction and Social Media: Embedded Barriers to Democratic Heritage. *International Journal of Heritage Studies*, 23(5), 408–420.

TED. (2017). Every Piece of Art You've Ever Wanted to See – Up Close and Searchable | Amit Sood. www.youtube.com/watch?v=CjB6DQGalU0.

The White House. (2021). Remarks by President Biden, Prime Minister Morrison of Australia, and Prime Minister Johnson of the United Kingdom Announcing the Creation of AUKUS, 15 September. www.whitehouse.gov/briefing-room/speeches-remarks/2021/09/15/remarks-by-president-biden-prime-minister-morrison-of-australia-and-prime-minister-johnson-of-the-united-kingdom-announcing-the-creation-of-aukus/.

Timmers, P. (2022). The Technological Construction of Sovereignty. In H. Werthner, E. Prem, E. A. Lee, and C. Ghezzi, eds., *Perspectives on Digital Humanism*. Cham: Springer International, pp. 213–218.

Tretter, E. (2011). The 'Value' of Europe: The Political Economy of Culture in the European Community. *Geopolitics*, 16(4), 926–948.

Trove Website. (2022a). Technical Specifications. https://trove.nla.gov.au/technical-specifications.

Trove Website. (2022b). Cultural Safety for First Australians. https://trove.nla.gov.au/help/using-trove/cultural-safety-first-australians.

Tuoi Tre News (TTN). (2021). Google Arts & Culture Brings Vivid, Energetic Vietnam to the World. https://tuoitrenews.vn/news/vietnam-life/vietnamese-culture/20210122/google-arts-culture-brings-vivid-energetic-vietnam-to-the-world/58938.html.

Turčalo, S., and Kulović, A. (2018). Contemporary Geopolitics and Digital Representations of Space. *Croatian International Relations Review*, 24(81), 7–22. https://doi.org/10.2478/cirr-2018-0001.

Udell, M. K. (2019). The Museum of the Infinite Scroll: Assessing the Effectiveness of Google Arts and Culture as a Virtual Tool for Museum Accessibility. *Master's Projects and Capstones*, 979. https://repository.usfca.edu/capstone/979.

UNESCO. (2009). Google and UNESCO Announce Alliance to Provide Virtual Visits of Several World Heritage Sites. https://bit.ly/2N7eHS8.

UNESCO. (2022). Discover the Memory of the World Register on Google Arts & Culture. www.unesco.org/en/articles/discover-memory-world-register-google-arts-culture.

Urry, J. (1995). *Consuming Places*. London: Routledge.

Valtysson, B. (2012). Europeana. *Information, Communication & Society*, 15(2), 151–170.

Valtysson, B. (2018). Camouflaged Culture: The 'Discursive Journey' of the EU's Cultural Programmes. *Croatian International Relations Review*, 24(82), 14–37.

Valtysson, B. (2020). *Digital Cultural Politics From Policy to Practice*. Cham: Palgrave MacMillan.

Van Dijck, J., Poell, T., and de Waal, M. (2018). *The Platform Society: Public Values in a Connective World*. Oxford: Oxford University Press.

Van Ham, P. (2008). Place Branding: The State of the Art. *The ANNALS of the American Academy of Political and Social Science*, 616(1), 126–149. https://doi.org/10.1177/0002716207312274.

Verhoeven, D. (2016). As Luck Would Have It: Serendipity and Solace in Digital Research Infrastructure. *Feminist Media Histories*, 2(1), 7–28.

Walker, C. (2017). Trove Atlas Project – Recommendations (Internal Report).

Wang, A. (2020). Rules of Engagement in the Global Arts City: The Case of The Substation in Singapore. In W. Byrnes, and A. Brkić, eds., *The Routledge Companion to Arts Management*. London: Routledge, pp. 187–202.

Wani, S. A., Ali, A., and Ganaie, S. A. (2019). The Digitally Preserved Old-aged Art, Culture and Artists. *PSU Research Review*, 3(2), 111–122. https://doi.org/10.1108/prr-08-2018-0026.

Werthner, H. (2022). Geopolitics, Digital Sovereignty . . . What's in a Word? In H. Werthner, E. Prem, E. A. Lee, and C. Ghezzi, eds., *Perspectives on Digital Humanism*. Cham: Springer International, pp. 241–248.

Widodo, J., Wong, Y.C. and Ismail, F. (2017). Digital Historic Urban Landscape Methodology for Heritage Impact Assessment of Singapore. *ISPRS Annals of the Photogrammetry, Remote Sensing and Spatial Information Sciences*, 4, 327–334.

Wikimedia. (2022). Characterizing Wikipedia Citation Usage: First Round of Analysis. https://meta.wikimedia.org/wiki/Research:Characterizing_Wikipedia_Citation_Usage/First_Round_of_Analysis.

Wilson-Barnao, C. (2017). How Algorithmic Cultural Rcommendation Influence the Marketing of Vultural collections. *Consumption Markets & Culture*, 20(6), 559–574. https://doi.org/10.1080/10253866.2017.1331910.

Wilson-Barnao, C. (2021). *Digital Access and Museums as Platforms*. London: Routledge. https://doi.org/10.4324/9780429298691-1.

Winter, T. (2020). Geocultural Power: China's Belt and Road Initiative. *Geopolitics*, 26(5), 1–24. https://doi.org/10.1080/14650045.2020.1718656.

Winter, T. (2021). Geocultural Power: China's Belt and Road Initiative. *Geopolitics*, 26(5), 1376–1399.

Winter, T. (2022a). Geocultural power and the Digital Silk Roads. *Environment and Planning D: Society and Space*, 40(5), 923–940. https://doi.org/10.1177/02637758221118569.

Winter, T. (2022b). Geocultural Diplomacy. *International Journal of Cultural Policy*, 28(4), 385–399. https://doi.org/10.1080/10286632.2021.1967943.

Winter, T. (2023). Heritage Diplomacy: An Afterword. *International Journal of Cultural Policy*, 29(1), 130–134. https://doi.org/10.1080/10286632.2022.2141728.

Wood, J. (2018). Unpublished Correspondence with Elizabeth Stainforth.

World Bank (WB) (n.d.a). Literacy Rate, Adult Total (% of People Ages 15 and Above) – Singapore | Data. *Data.worldbank.org*. https://data.worldbank.org/indicator/SE.ADT.LITR.ZS?locations=SG&name_desc=true.

World Bank (WB). (n.d.). Individuals Using the Internet (% of Population) – Singapore | Data. *Data.worldbank.org*. https://data.worldbank.org/indicator/IT.NET.USER.ZS?locations=SG.

World Bank (WB). (n.d.c). GDP (Current US$) – Singapore | Data. *Data.worldbank.org*. https://data.worldbank.org/indicator/NY.GDP.MKTP.CD?locations=SG.

World Bank (WB). (2019). Vietnam's Economy Expanded by 6.8 Percent in 2019 but Reforms are Needed to Unleash the Potential of Capital Markets. www.worldbank.org/en/news/press-release/2019/12/17/vietnams-economy-expanded-by-68-percent-in-2019-but-reforms-are-needed-to-unleash-the-potential-of-capital-markets.

World Economic Forum (WEF). (2015). Which Languages Rule the Internet? www.weforum.org/agenda/2015/11/which-languages-rule-the-internet/.

Yeo, S. (2016). Geopolitics of Search: Google versus China? *Media, Culture & Society*, 38(4), 591–605. https://doi.org/10.1177/0163443716643014.

Yeo, S. (2018). Access Now, But for Whom and at What Cost? Information, Communication & Society, 23(4), 588–604. https://doi.org/10.1080/1369118x.2018.1529192.

Yue, A. (2006). Cultural Governance and Creative Industries in Singapore. *International Journal of Cultural Policy*, 12(1), 17–33. https://doi.org/10.1080/10286630600613176.

Zheleva, E. (2011). 5 Questions with Amit Sood and James David from Google Art. *Social Media Week*. https://socialmediaweek.org/blog/2011/07/5-questions-with-amit-sood-and-james-david-from-googleart/.

Zuboff, S. (2019). *The Age of Surveillance Capitalism: The Fight for a Human Future at the New Frontier of Power*. New York: Profile Books.

Cambridge Elements

Critical Heritage Studies

Kristian Kristiansen
University of Gothenburg

Michael Rowlands
UCL

About the Series

This series focuses on the recently established field of Critical Heritage Studies. Interdisciplinary in character, it brings together contributions from experts working in a range of fields, including cultural management, anthropology, archaeology, politics, and law. The series will include volumes that demonstrate the impact of contemporary theoretical discourses on heritage found throughout the world, raising awareness of the acute relevance of critically analysing and understanding the way heritage is used today to form new futures.

Cambridge Elements

Critical Heritage Studies

Elements in the Series

Heritage Justice
Charlotte Joy

Patrimonialities: Heritage vs. Property
Valdimar Tr. Hafstein and Martin Skrydstrup

Heritage Tourism: From Problems to Possibilities
Yujie Zhu

Construing Cultural Heritage: The Stagings of an Artist: The Case of Ivar Arosenius
Mats Malm

Native Americans in British Museums: Living Histories
Jack Davy

Understanding Islam at European Museums
Magnus Berg and Klas Grinell

Ethnographic Returns: Memory Processes and Archive Film
Anne Gustavsson

Global Heritage, Religion, and Secularism
Trinidad Rico

Heritage Making and Migrant Subjects in the Deindustrialising Region of the Latrobe Valley
Alexandra Dellios

Heritage and Design: Ten Portraits from Goa (India)
Pamila Gupta

Heritage, Education and Social Justice
Veysel Apaydin

Geopolitics of Digital Heritage
Natalia Grincheva and Elizabeth Stainforth

A full series listing is available at: www.cambridge.org/CHSE

Printed in the United States
by Baker & Taylor Publisher Services